What a performance gem! Kirsten understands the deepest parts of what matters to performance, and her book *When Grit Is Not Enough* is an incredible guide to bringing out our best performance and our best selves. She has uncovered the hidden tools to deliver on the most challenging goals with less pain and more gain! She has brilliantly written this in a way that is valuable to the most experienced performer and the new aspiring young performers at the start of their journey. But the book's brilliance lies in the fact this is written to benefit leaders, directors, coaches, scientists, parents and families ... all of us committing our energy and heart to release the potential in future performers. What a relief to read her words and know her tools are the secret to achieving better with more fulfilment and more meaning. Kirsten highlights standout actionable insights about purpose and passion, "smarter quitting," reducing the drama and increasing the advantage. If you are like me and have been involved in numerous Olympic Games and are looking for a toolbox to unleash the real talents in future leaders and performers, then this book is a must-read!

Richard Young, PhD
Former head of innovation for Great Britain and New Zealand Sport
and 10 Olympics uncovering the keys to repeat medal enabling systems

Many aspects of the human condition (personality traits, stressful environments, thought processes, emotional responsivity) are double-edged swords leading to both pleasure and pain. What happens when our successes and victories, in life and on the playing fields, lean toward the pyrrhic? Such observations and questions are at the heart of Dr. Kirsten Peterson's wonderful new book, and she should know, having been at the forefront of performance psychology working with the United States Olympic and Paralympic Committee and the Australian Institute of Sport for over 20 years. Storytelling is a core feature of the book, from the demanding socio-cultural narratives that permeate sports environments to our harsh internal critic's reminders about how we are never quite good enough. This book reminded me of Brené Brown's observation, "You either walk inside your story and own it, or you stand outside your story and hustle for your worthiness." Peterson's book will be helpful for many sports people to discover how to "walk inside."

Professor Mark B. Andersen
Halmstad University, Sweden

Elite sport so often touts unrelenting grit as the key to success but rarely sheds light on the steps to take when grit becomes ineffective. Dr. Peterson's insight into the complexities of grit in elite athletes is unmatched given her years of experience working with Olympic- and Paralympic-level athletes across the globe. This is a must-read to help elite athletes achieve their best and live a life worth living on and off the field.

Rachael Flatt, 2010 Olympic Figure Skater; US Figure Skating
Board of Directors; Athlete Mental Health Advocate/Researcher

When you want to be the best, you need to learn from the best. In my over 20 years working with elite performers in business, I have learned that a mindset without a skillset gets you nowhere. Dr. Kirsten Peterson leverages her expertise to deliver on what people need most, a solution to when grit isn't enough. This book includes tips, tools, skills, and insights that can help people be their best when they may be feeling their worst. Kirsten helps us relearn our relationship with mental toughness and offers a new way of putting in effort. I highly recommend this book to every executive and person who is looking to get an edge and sustain optimal performance in work and in life.

Rob Fazio, PhD
Author of *BullyProof*
Leadership Psychologist with OnPoint Advising

Grit was never enough for me to become an Olympian; if only I knew this back then, I would have worked even smarter (and less "harder"), striving for more effective, "clean" effort and performance. Kirsten shares decades of experience with athletes of the highest level, providing essential reading for any athlete, coach or support staff navigating performance demands in today's volatile world.

Dr. Trevor Brown
(PhD, Cognitive Neuroscience)
Australian Olympian, Athens 2004

I first met Dr. Kirsten Peterson at the US Olympic Training Center in Colorado Springs, CO in the late 1980s. We were both Sport Science Research Assistants learning about the exciting world of elite sport. Years later when I was working at the Australian Institute of Sport, I introduced Kirsten to my colleagues, who quickly recognized her brilliance and offered her a position leading the AIS Performance Sport Psychology program.

Over the past 30 years I have watched Kirsten work her magic with elite athletes and coaches while at the same time remaining connected to the science of high-performance sport. I have often thought, "Kirsten, you should write a book." Well, here it is.

The advice contained within this book is authentic and fresh. I am sure anyone with an open mind who wishes to pursue extraordinary goals can benefit from Kirsten's pragmatic insights, which have emerged from her time supporting talented athletes as they prepared for some of the most intense sporting events the world has to offer. The Greek Stoic Philosopher Epictetus is believed to have said, "It's not what happens to you but how you react to it that matters." Kirsten focuses on this central theme and gives advice on how to "get it right" but also insights on how to cope with the inevitable realities of hardship and disappointment.

All too often, when experts are asked questions about whether a particular intervention or methodology works for elite athletes, they answer, "it depends". Kirsten goes one step further and takes the time to illuminate why some popular approaches don't always work and what to do when hope is lost.

In contrast to so many self-help books written by passionate academics outlining one single approach to achieving greatness, Kirsten has prepared a performance support manual that focuses on priorities and perspectives. As a sport scientist who has interacted with many coaches and athletes who are well-prepared to persevere but are not always ready to refine their approach when times are tough, I found worthwhile advice in every chapter.

This book was inspired by a global pandemic but has been conceptually in preparation since Kirsten first started working with Olympians in Colorado Springs. Within this book you will gain the collective wisdom that only comes from spending decades helping talented individuals pursue lofty goals. You will learn about grit, uncertainty, acceptance, friendship, passion, purpose and service. I loved the final product, and I am sure you will too. Well done, Kirsten!

Dr. David T. Martin
Honorary Professor, Australian Catholic University; Chief Scientist and
Director of Performance, Performance Health Sciences, LLC

In my 20 years as Team USA Women's Wrestling's National Team Coach, I have had few books that have helped me analyse and work through the struggles to be successful in sport or life. I wish I had this knowledge decades ago. In this book you will find concepts like the "Aware - Accept – Act" sequence that allowed me to better set myself in tough times and uncertainty. This is a book that I will recommend not only to the athletes on our national team but also to all the coaches in our development pipeline. Thank you, Kirsten, for sharing your wisdom!

Terry Steiner
USA Wrestling Women's National Team Coach

I wish I'd had this book as a reference when I started my sport psychology career, or even earlier, when I was an athlete.

Each chapter communicates in a way that connects. The analogies and metaphors really bring thoughts and ideas to life. The last chapter resonates—the distinction between "clean effort" and "dirty effort" many of us will identify with—e.g., working hard versus working smart.

In *When Grit Is Not Enough*, Kirsten has created a very practical guide where every thought-provoking chapter enables us to become more aware of what drives and motivates us and influences our choices as performers.

Patsy Tremayne, PhD, FAPS
Sport and Performance Psychologist and Medical Psychologist

Kirsten takes her wealth of experience and knowledge in the high-performance sport and sport psychology spaces, asks the good questions, contemplates critical aspects of being human, and brings new information and ideas on how to enhance our own skills and knowledge in such a unique time. She is highly skilled at taking the research and putting it into real, practical terms, which is a gift to those of us in need of research translation. She makes the case of why one can't rely on grit alone and provides 'grit-enhancing insight', building upon Duckworth's research in this area and giving us more tools and ways to consider grit. This book will be invaluable to those seeking to continue to improve and build awareness around health, well-being and performance for all humans.

Christine Bolger
Associate Director, Coaching Education
US Olympic and Paralympic Committee

To Tom,

Thanks so much for your support and encouragement – of both my business, as well as this book! May all your life adventures require only just enough grit. :)

Happy Reading,
Kirstin

WHEN

REWORKING MINDSET AND PURPOSE FOR

GRIT

EASIER EFFORT IN HARD TIMES

IS NOT ENOUGH

KIRSTEN PETERSON, PhD

A catalogue record for this book is available from the National Library of Australia

First published in 2022 by Hambone Publishing
Melbourne, Australia

Editing by Laura E. Larson and Kathleen Larson Florio
Typesetting and Design by David W. Edelstein
Cover Design by Tanja Prokop
Back cover photo by Karlee Holland

For information about this title, contact:
Kirsten Peterson
kirsten@kirstenpetersonconsulting.com
www.kirstenpetersonconsulting.com

ISBN 978-1-922357-45-8 (paperback)
ISBN 978-1-922357-46-5 (eBook)

To Dad

*my first and best coach, a man who always put character
before competence—my first grit instructor!—
and whose boundless love and encouragement made me
believe that I had a book in me.*

ACKNOWLEDGEMENTS

To my family, first, my husband Dan, an inveterate reader of all my writing and whose unwavering support of me, my career, and this latest book-writing adventure made all of this possible. To my daughter Mika, who, through her gritty efforts and ceaseless bravery as she moves through the world of young adulthood, inspires me to be a better mother and human every day.

The athletes and coaches I have had the privilege to work with throughout my career whose lives, struggles, wins, and losses underpin every word of this book.

Angela Duckworth, for writing the book *Grit* that built the foundation from which I could launch this tome, and for her generous sharing of her time and insights.

Laura Larson, for a lifetime of the firmest of friendship, her ceaseless bolstering and encouragement, never mind her witty and impeccable editing.

Kathleen Larson Florio, for her wonderful and informative copy editing and wry sense of humor.

Tanja Prokop, my cover designer, for hanging in there through numerous and no doubt pedantic tweaks to her design.

Karlee Holland, my photographer, for making me look better than I deserve.

The wonderful folks at Hambone Publishing.

Jenny Magee, for early book mind-mapping help and for enthusiastically endorsing my ideas in their infancy.

My reader, Jane Gorrie.

Interviewees: Scott Brennan, Mike Candrea, Cindra Kamphoff, Bronwen Knox, and Mike Kohn, whose generosity and wisdom shared through hours of interviews brought this book to life.

Tristan Gale, for graciously allowing me to include my recollections of our work together in this book.

The wonderful community at Thought Leaders Business School, from the faculty to my beyond-wonderful fellow practitioners who have made my journey up to and through this book both believable and much easier.

CONTENTS

FOREWORD

Back in 1994, I found myself as the lone sport psychologist at the United States Olympic Committee, tasked with building up the program in response to the growing interest in and growing need for sport psychology. Knowing the first hire I made was the most important, I asked older and wiser leaders how you choose an essential colleague. I was given the wise advice to "pick someone smarter and more capable than you." As many would tell you, this is not a very high bar! However, as I looked over the applications, one rose clearly to the top, a young sport psychologist named Dr. Kirsten Peterson, and I told myself not to be afraid to hire the best. From the time Kirsten arrived 'til she left, our sport psychology team was very successful and grew dramatically, in large part due to her many accomplishments. When Kirsten chose to leave, to lead a similar Olympic sport psychology program in Australia, I knew she would be successful, and I knew Australia's gain was our giant loss. One key loss for us was her practicality.

In the world of sport and performance psychology over the last 40 years, there have been many theoretical models that have gained favor and interest at various times. Models and theories are useful, and perhaps even essential for providing a compass to get from where you are in your work to where you want to be. On the other hand, a compass without a map or a keen knowledge of the current territory isn't nearly as useful. With some of the world's upheavals over the last three years changing the landscape so dramatically, Kirsten has written a book that recognizes that changing your approach may be the best way to keep moving forward.

As I read Kirsten's book, I found myself nodding my head in agreement, time after time. The world's recent experience with Covid sharpened the key messages in this book. Toughness isn't enough; stubbornness isn't enough when obstacles are not only enormous, but also constantly changing. Grit is great, but sometimes performers must move beyond. Understanding that adaptability, resilience, flexibility, and timely use of mental skills is always a challenge, even in normal times but especially so in uncertain times. And in my experience, moments of great pressure increase the odds of uncertainty and increase the need for the kind of strategies and skills Kirsten talks about in her valuable, enjoyable, and practical book.

Having had the privilege of working side-by-side with Kirsten, I can vouch for her skill in understanding performance problems, coming up with solutions, helping to make those solutions easy to understand and practical to achieve. I know her approach works, because I have seen it work over and over, across a wide variety of individuals and contexts. I have seen her remind an athlete of specific strategies just before they won an Olympic medal and the athlete thanking her in tears afterwards. But it's not just with world-class athletes where her approach is useful. Today Kirsten applies the same practical skills and approach in working with a wide variety of people, from athletes to high performers in business, the military, and other arenas. I took many lessons from *When Grit Is Not Enough* that I will use in my work, and I am sure that readers will find a wide variety of thought-provoking ideas and examples that will be useful in their lives as well.

Sean McCann, PhD
Senior Sport Psychologist,
United States Olympic and Paralympic Committee

INTRODUCTION:
THE COST OF UNCERTAINTY

We are living through a period of uncertainty in proportions not seen since World War II. Because of the Covid-19 pandemic, we have coped with massive lifestyle shifts brought on by lockdowns, work-situation changes, and home-schooling children, followed by the longer-term ripple effects caused by competition cancellations, delays, and the more immediate and changing demands caused by a virus with variants that flare up at will.

For sport, this unpredictable and sometimes chaotic reality has meant that the structures that we have traditionally relied and thrived on—established competition schedules, stable training environments, ease of travel to train or compete—are more difficult to achieve, delayed, or absent. In addition, this is the first time in the history of the modern Olympics that we have had a five-year quadrennium—uncharted territory. For athletes, this scenario has meant, at times, isolated and substandard training, uncertainty about schedules, decision fatigue, and a lack of clarity and purpose. For coaches, it has meant less financial stability; more complex planning; concerns about employment and family; coping with distressed, less motivated athletes; and trying to judge athlete fitness from disrupted training. Staff who were tasked with caring for the sport organisation as a whole have been stretched to continue to provide resources, advice, or support to distressed athletes and coaches.

It's seductive to think that "once this is all over, we can return to normal," but just watching the virus variants emerging, raging new hot spots, and persistent challenges with vaccines and vaccine supply-chain issues puts us all on notice that the wait for "normal" may be a long one. The reality is that some changes are here to stay, while in other ways the ground may keep shifting for the foreseeable future. Thinking we may ever get back to what passes for comfortable stability and predictability is unrealistic. This can be a hard "unlearning" of those tried-and-true chestnuts athletes had to learn in order to go from good to great. It's hard, even counterproductive, to keep trying harder or persevering with a single-minded focus along a road when the bridge ahead has been washed away.

Athletes are told to trust their coaches, stick to the plan, when to train, when to train harder, and when to recover. National training centres and training camps provide opportunities for athletes to come together and gauge their progress against their competitors, and for coaches to know who's doing what and how well. Sport science staff have the opportunity to interact with everyone, adding expertise and service along the way. Effective elite sport relies on systems and oversight to take athletes from good to great as efficiently as possible. Here's what used to work.

In the environment:

- Structured, periodised, proven training programs. Coaches coach, and smart, dedicated athletes listen and follow.
- Financial plans developed, in place, and secure. Coaches have contracts, and athletes get their stipends (if they are ranked highly enough).
- Organised activities/competitions. The calendar is there for all to see.

For the individual:

- We are mentally tough. Go hard; go harder.
- We know what our goals are: make the team, make the squad, go to Worlds, and win at the Olympics.
- We know what our timeframes are, how long we have to do the work, and commit to the plan.

It turns out that we can't always rely on what used to be controllable: our programs, our financial plans, our competition schedules. The previously prescribed path no longer serves us and in some cases has been taken away.

Grit—that balance of passion and perseverance that keeps us going when times are tough, grinding through discomfort—may not serve us when we don't even know if today's path will exist tomorrow.

For athletes, it has been a time of fear and uncertainty, lack of motivation, and even some soul-searching about whether the journey is worth it anymore, with other life obligations increasingly pressing in. The year-long delay of the 2020 Olympics was actually fortuitous for injured athletes who were given the gift of time to complete their rehabilitations. On the other hand, it was downright gutting for those athletes who had calibrated their training to reach peak physical fitness and had actually been selected to compete for the 2020 Olympic team, only to have to do a rewind of the entire process a year later. Still other athletes wondered, "Do I have it in me to go another whole year?" and decided against it.

Coaches have been worried. "How do I coach effectively in this time? My career is about producing winners; but without competitions, with only fractured and suboptimal training opportunities, how do I do that? How do I evaluate my athletes' fitness, coach appropriately, or even select an Olympic team with so little data?"

This book examines how we can change our thinking, the way we relate to ourselves, our colleagues, and the athletes we work with to increase not only our effectiveness but our well-being. It will also check in with our purpose—for ourselves, why we do what we do and how we apply that in our work in sport, with an eye for better directing our efforts.

It's All About Engagement

Another way to think about this is that this is a book about *engagement*. In times of chronic uncertainty and change, people—athletes, coaches, and staff—can and will react in a number of different ways that can impact their ability to function and cope well. When we are feeling most threatened by a situation, our instinct is to fight, freeze, or flee. That is, if the situation is overwhelming or really unpredictable, leaving it—or disengaging—is the fastest way to relieve our negative feelings. On the other hand, when organizations and leaders respond empathically and appropriately to meet athletes where they are and provide targeted and relevant support, not only are athletes more likely to remain engaged in that moment, but their goodwill for the organisation increases.

By way of example, we saw athletes leave national team programs in response to a lack of flexibility in some sports' processes as Covid decimated the normal course of business through 2020. If an athlete is on the brink of leaving and the goal is to retain them, then empathic support, rather than a rigid adherence to protocol, may well be the way to go. I showcase an example of this kind of thinking in Chapter 8.

This book's reason for being is all about the idea of enhancing engagement, even when the future is uncertain and plans have been thrown out and rewritten numerous times. How do we stay engaged and productive? How do we support those we work with and lead to do the same?

If we think of the process of engagement as a ladder (see Figure 1.1), on the left-hand side of the ladder are the states of being I have observed in athletes and coaches as the pandemic raged. At the bottom rung is disengagement, when the costs of staying outweigh the benefits. If retaining talent is the goal, this is a lose-lose proposition. At the next level are those individuals who may choose to stay but are compromised by a perpetual sense of outrage at the injustices of their situation.

These rigid thinkers fight the reality they are presented with, vacillating between anger and fear. Next up is the indecisive individual—the person who hesitates to "pull the trigger" on a decision for fear it's not the best one or that circumstances will render it moot anyway, and then what?

Both rigidity and indecision are understandable but less effective ways to respond to uncertainty. At the next step of the ladder, however, we see a shift in thinking toward an orientation that, if not actually more effective, helps the individual suffer less. This is when curiosity kicks in. Individuals at this stage step away from seeing the uncertain reality as only a threat and start considering what opportunities might exist. And finally, at the top of the ladder is that fully engaged individual, more prone to embracing the situation as it exists, more likely to seek solutions and work collaboratively.

It is equally important to recognise that, given these different reactions to uncertainty, coaches, leaders, and staff can increase the likelihood of engagement by offering differentiated responses, as shown on the right-hand side of the ladder. When someone is on the brink of disengagement, their sense of hope and agency is likely to be low and they may benefit from a more supportive response. Rigidity, on the other hand, can benefit from leaders providing alternative ways to think about the situation. Those who are indecisive or confused may respond positively to someone providing a more structured approach that helps them settle into a productive way forward. Contrast this with the curious person, who may resonate more with someone who can help shape their curiosity but not stamp it out. With the engaged, the image is of the leader walking alongside, guiding but not getting in the way.

This book provides the tools to help athletes, coaches, and staff understand the different ways people respond to uncertainty and change—the left-hand side of the ladder—as well as how we can best help ourselves and those we serve to go from "out" to "in," as represented on the right-hand side of the ladder.

	What They Are SAYING	How We Can HELP
Engaged	*I'm in.*	Be a partner
Curious	*What are the opportunities?*	Offer counsel
Indecisive	*What do I do now?*	Provide structure
Rigid	*It has to be this way!*	Give perspective
Disengaged	*I'm out.*	Offer support

Figure 1.1. Reactions and Responses to Uncertainty:
From Disengaged to Engaged

Alternatively, we can think of our ability to cope effectively through uncertainty as being on one or more of these attitudinal spectrums:

Disengaged	Engaged
Rigid	Flexible
Indecisive	Planful
Closed Off	Curious

Figure 1.2. Attitudinal Spectrums

That is, we could ask individuals to pinpoint their state of mind at any given time by indicating where they land on each of these spectrums. I may be highly engaged, but my rigidity in thinking thwarts my ability to respond effectively when plans are changing rapidly. Another individual may be somewhat engaged but struggled because her need for advance planning—a nonstarter for months in 2020–2021—meant she was having to shift her training on very short notice, over and over.

The point is not only that people respond to uncertainty and change in different ways, but also that this difference should dictate the support we provide. Moreover, both people's responses—and our support—can and will change over time.

We can't influence the uncertainty, but there are things we can do to lessen our individual and sometimes even collective fights against it.

How This Book Is Organised

This book provides relevant insights and skills for this uniquely challenging time but at the same time readies us for whatever new normal(s) await. It is divided into four sections, starting from the inside out.

Section 1: Introduction to Grit. To be clear, I have no beef with grit. There are times when having more of it can game-change one's journey and be a catalyst to keep going toward life's Big Goals when the going gets tough. I unpack grit's bright side in Chapter 1, why this concept remains vital and important for many of us under the right circumstances. I then discuss the pitfalls of grit in Chapter 2: what it looks and feels like when grit is overused or applied mindlessly in the face of changing circumstance.

Section 2: Introduction to Mindset. In Chapter 3, readers will learn about mind and brain realities and how evolution has shaped the way we interact with uncertainty. The good news is that we can work with our evolutionary attitudinal tendencies to become more balanced and nimble. Chapter 4 discusses the idea of "presence"—the ability to "be here now"—and its importance as a foundational mental skill in times of uncertainty. Being more present more regularly often gives us more agency and has the potential to make us happier. Chapter 5 showcases the power of acceptance and awareness as precursors for better, smarter action. Chapter 6 focuses on the relationship we all have with ourselves and how to shift that relationship for increased resilience.

Section 3: Introduction to Purpose. In Chapter 7, I take on the idea of passion—part of Angela Duckworth's original conception of grit—and how, while it can take us part of the way to grit, can also fail us. In Chapter 8, I discuss the utility of having a purpose that keeps us pointed in the right direction, how this can make our efforts more efficient and accurate no matter what is happening around us, and how to craft our own "fit for purpose" purpose. In Chapter 9, I move from an individual orientation of purpose ("What's *my* purpose?") to "How do I serve others?" This shift, from personal to service-oriented, can often add weight and import to our sense of purpose.

Section 4: Introduction to Effort. If effort is the behavioural personification of grit, then it behooves us to pay attention to and get right the why, how, and direction of our efforts. Chapter 10 discusses what happens when our perseverance runs amok and our efforts get less effective. Chapter 11 dives into the paradoxical subject of quitting—an action that on the surface can be seen as diametrically opposed to grit, but that is also at times not only desirable but necessary. Chapter 12 offers suggestions for how we can think and behave in the interest of effort that "burns clean"—the kind of effort that takes us where we *really* want to go . . . with the least effort necessary.

PART I
INTRODUCTION TO GRIT

Confession time. When I started writing this book, I hadn't even read Angela Duckworth's best-selling book on the concept—grit—that I was arguing wasn't enough. Here's why. At the time of her book's arrival on the scene, circa 2016, I was sceptical about adding another term to the mental high-performance lexicon—yet another way that we could berate ourselves or others over a lack of perceived mental effort when the going got tough. Folks in the elite sport world used to call this a lack of character, or mental weakness, more recently adopting "mental toughness" as the term for that which differentiated the doers from the pretenders. None of these, in my experience, accurately represented why some of us struggle to persevere, and the use of these phrases only served to make the underachievers feel worse about themselves. Did we need yet another shaming label to put on athletes who didn't meet some imagined standard? No, thank you.

But the term *grit* grew in popularity, with everyone and their grandmother starting to marvel at the prospect of legions of grittier athletes ready for any challenge. With a sigh, I defaulted to watching Duckworth's TED Talk, where she described the *why* and *what* that underpinned her research into grit. At the time, Duckworth was unsure of how to teach people to be grittier, which made sense, given the developmental state of her theory—a retroactive exploration of what appeared to differentiate those she called "grit paragons" from the rest of us. This did little to warm me to the concept. I had little time for or interest in theories that didn't come with pragmatic tools to help me in my work with athletes.

Then came 2020, when Covid hit and I started to notice how a portion of people I would have thought of as gritty as all get-out started to falter. The chronic and deep uncertainty brought on by the pandemic meant that many a well-developed plan, many a tried-and-true routine was suddenly useless. And it was a portion of those people who typically were the ones I *didn't* worry about—athletes who always got the job done, coaches who just kept motoring though—who appeared to struggle the most, while others were able to flex, bend, and respond, and get on with some sort of business even if it wasn't the same prototype of business as usual.

Wanting to understand the differences between those who suffered versus those who, if not thrived, were able to more easily "go with the flow," I started writing this book. I wanted to share what I knew from my work with gritty athletes and coaches—when things worked and when they did not. I wanted people to have fit-for-purpose tools to augment or even (heaven forbid) replace their grit.

While this was happening, I was forced, throughout my writing, to confront the uncomfortable reality brought on by trying to describe a concept I hadn't fully researched. I was also worried I might be selling grit short. Who was I to say when grit's not enough if I didn't have more than a passing acquaintance with the concept? Worse, what if Duckworth had already explored and solved the problem of what to do if you had too much grit or overused it? All of which compelled me—with another sigh—to buy and actually read the book *Grit: The Power of Passion and Perseverance*.

Grit's a big book, no lie. My version topped out at 440 pages. Yet once I sat down to read it, I was hooked. Duckworth uses stories and her prolific research program and collaborations across numerous domains to shed light on what underpins the process of achievement—particularly achievement of goals and outcomes that are long in the making. Descriptions of the factors that correlate with grit are interwoven with stories from "grit paragons." She even provides a self-assessment to determine how gritty you are, and I was happy to discover that I'm in the 90th percentile; that is, I'm grittier than 90 percent of her sampled adults.

But I could not find anything in the book that concerned itself with people who overused grit or had "too much" of it, aside from a couple cautionary paragraphs in the concluding chapter. There, Duckworth postulated (after admitting that she had yet to research this question) that, like many traits, an inverted-U relationship might exist for grit. That is, too little of it makes it ineffective as an agent, while too much can get you into trouble. She quickly went on to blunt this reasoning, joking that she wished she lived in a reality where everyone was persisting with their long-held goals. Nor did she find evidence of folks wishing they had less grit. She thought that there might be exceptions to this trend but that those exceptions are rare.

She also addresses this same question in the FAQ section on her website:

> **Can you be too gritty?** I don't have any data that suggests there are drawbacks to being extremely gritty. Indeed, at the very top of the Grit Scale, I typically find individuals who are tremendously successful and also satisfied with their lives. However, as I mention in the concluding chapter of the book, this doesn't mean we should entirely dismiss the possibility of "too much grit." In particular, I think you can be too stubborn about mid-level and low-level goals. You can throw good money after bad on particular projects that will never make sense. You can be blind to possibilities you hadn't originally anticipated. Still, I think these problems are mostly about lower-level goals that are in service of your high-level goals—those abstract and enduring concerns that I describe in Chapter Four. For me, my very highest-level goal is to use psychological science to help kids thrive. That's my mission statement, and I can't think of anything that would make me give up on it. (AngelaDuckworth.com/qa/#faq-60)

To say that I was relieved to not have discovered more substance about the problem of too much grit was an understatement—at least for my book's sake. It made sense that in Angela Duckworth's world—helping kids to thrive—the overarching goal would be to help kids build their grit, not get rid of it. But now I was really curious about my contention that, indeed, grit, while a superpower for some folks, could also prove to be their kryptonite if misplayed or overused.

So I asked Duckworth herself. I found a way to reach her via the internet. She has formed her own company, Character Lab, with the following mission statement: "To advance science that helps kids thrive." I emailed her with my observations and questions about what the "far end" of grit might look like and asked if she'd be willing to comment. I was gobsmacked when less than an hour later she wrote me back and even agreed to an interview.

We ended up having a great chat. Angela (I reckon I can call her that now) is interested in understanding the limits of grit, but given her emphasis on developing it in kids, she has not devoted much time or attention to the idea. So it was more of us doing some educated guessing around what could be going on for those who are on the far end of the grit spectrum. Here's where we landed.

The pursuit of one's passion is best done mindfully as well as in a way that is persevering. That is, we agreed that it was those folks who did not allow themselves to question the ongoing efficacy of their plans that were more at risk for persevering past the point of usefulness. Angela characterised this tendency as a sort of "myopia," getting stuck in the daily weeds of a gritty pursuit and seeing nothing but that. We agreed that, for people of this ilk, it would be vital to do some periodic perspective shifting, to lift one's head above the grind and take a look around. Am I heading in the right direction? Do I even know what that means anymore?

Grit does not mean the pursuit of one's goals "at the expense of one's body or health." Angela was clear that grit and mental toughness are not the same, despite popular literature often conflating the two concepts. In her view, being "mentally tough" means that people persist in their endeavours with a disregard for their mental or physical health, while the same cannot be said for grit. Honestly, however, whatever term one uses, the potential for misuse of tough-mindedness (or grit) is real, and this is one of the reasons I wrote this book: to make us smarter about how we apply ourselves so that we are less likely to get spit out the other end, suffering from burnout, exhaustion, or disillusion.

In the meantime, I see this book as coming from the concept of grit from the far side of the concept's spectrum, as it were. That is, while there is a compelling case to be made for helping people—children especially—understand how grit works and how to nurture it, gritty people can benefit from knowing certain things. These include knowing what to do when simply being gritty is not enough to get them where they want to go; how to know when to deviate from or even quit a gritty path, if necessary; key mindset elements that can augment grit in times of uncertainty; and understanding effort and how to wield it more skilfully.

If you feel like you don't have any or just want more grit, read Angela Duckworth's incredible book, *Grit: The Power of Passion and Perseverance*, which will teach you what it is and ways to nurture it. If, on the other hand, you have always prided yourself on your grit but find yourself being less effective or happy with your efforts, this book's for you.

Section 1 kicks off with Chapter 1, "What Is Grit," in which I drill down on the basic concepts underpinning grit, based on Angela Duckworth's book and ideas. In Chapter 2, "The Downside of Grit," I spell out the conditions that could potentially undermine grit. This "up and down" of the grit landscape informs the strategies laid out in the rest of the book.

1   WHAT IS GRIT?

The term *grit* was coined by Angela Duckworth (2016) to explain how it was that, in challenging situations, or even most of the time, the people who had the most talent did not always win the day. In domains that ranged from elementary school to the Scripps National Spelling Bee, West Point, sales, Olympic sport and beyond, a portion of people succeeded who defied the conventional "talent is everything" wisdom. Duckworth's interviews revealed that while talent did play a role, it was not the only thing needed for success. Talented people who also persevered through obstacles and over time, past setbacks and failure, were the ones more likely to succeed.

The problem is, despite our collective protestations that we value effort and trying more than natural talent, we are biased to prefer the opposite. Duckworth described a research study in which people listened to pieces of piano music played either by someone with great talent or by someone who had worked hard to develop their abilities. Despite the fact that both pieces were performed by the same pianist, respondents rated the "talented musician's" piece more highly.

There appear to be a few mechanisms that lead to this bias. We enjoy talent in the same way we enjoy watching a magician. We enjoy being entertained and even fooled, as it allows us to believe in magic and the divine. No one less than the famous German philosopher Friedrich Nietzsche argued against our tendency to idolise giftedness and in favour of its underpinning industriousness. If we relegate achievement to those with talent, says Nietzsche (1878/1986), we are also able to protect our own egos. No use any of us trying if it all comes down to talent anyway.

> *Because we think well of ourselves, but in no way expect that we could ever make the sketch to a painting by Raphael or a scene like one in a play by Shakespeare, we convince ourselves that the ability to do so is quite excessively wonderful, a quite uncommon accident, or, if we still have a religious sensibility, a grace from above.*
> (Nietzsche & Hollingdale, 1878/1986, p. 162)

The issue is that behind almost every great talent there lurks a very hard worker and a long history of effort. We just don't get to see that part. Consider the Olympics. When I talk to sports fans about what makes watching the Games so compelling, the answer often is about getting to see a slew of different sports on offer, watching talent in action in dozens of different formats. You might not know much about the sport, but you can tell that there's a hell of a lot of talent on display, particularly in that the Games often showcase the world's best against the rest, and some of the rest aren't all that great, as it turns out. The range of abilities on display underscores the contrast of the best in the world versus, well, the merely pretty good. And in the end, it appears that talent usually wins out. What we don't hear about or see nearly as much is the day-in, day-out training regimens, strength training, flexibility work, and regular body and mind maintenance that underpin those podium appearances. Great athletes often riff a version of this C. S. Lewis quote as they mentor the up-and-comers:

 *Integrity involves doing the right thing,
even when no one is watching.*

Being excellent in anything involves a heck of a lot of thankless, behind-the-scenes work.

The same could be said about grit. In the world of elite sport, talent generally just gets you a seat at the table. For most athletes, there's so much more to the story, much of which is beyond the scope of this book, focusing as it does on the *psychology* of achievement. Coaching, training facilities, equipment, nutrition, and a host of other details all contribute. In the end, though, it's about what you *do* with your talent that takes most athletes from good to great.

Effort Counts Twice

Turns out that, in Duckworth's formulation, while talent does play a role in many gritty journeys, it's one's *effort* that makes the critical difference. In her model portraying grit, effort counts twice:

$$Talent \times Effort = Skill$$
$$Skill \times Effort = Achievement$$

Moreover, it's not just that *first* effort, which we all are familiar with come each new year when we plunk down cold, hard cash for that gym membership that gathers dust after January. Here's how Duckworth (2016) describes it:

> Staying on the treadmill is one thing, and I do think it's related to staying true to our commitments even when we are not comfortable. **But getting back on the treadmill the next day,** eager to try again, is in my view even more reflective of grit. Because when you don't come back the next day—when you permanently turn your back on a commitment—your effort plummets to zero. (pp. 60–61, emphasis added)

Duckworth points out that the less talented individuals who put in the work over time are actually *building* their talent, adding that they will eventually outperform their more talented but less industrious counterparts.

In case it is not obvious, it is also worth noting that the quality of effort matters. It is less about the intensity of effort and all about consistency over time. People who throw themselves headlong into new endeavours, flame out, and repeat those frantic efforts in something else do not meet the criteria for grit, which is reserved for those endeavours that require time, sustained action, and loyalty to the cause.

Passion + Perseverance

Duckworth sees grit as the combination of these two under-pinning concepts. Gritty people describe having an abiding interest in their endeavour; this interest is the passion part of the equation. Note the qualifier "abiding," which is the difference between a passing fancy and that strong interest that keeps you awake at night and has you thinking about the same things the next morning.

In this formulation, it's worth repeating that, contrary to the popular notion of passion being all about the intensity of the attraction, if you were to take the grit scale, the questions that generate your passion score ask you to reflect on how steadily you hold onto your goals over time. Even Duckworth wonders about her choice of words here, and I agree that there may be better ways to describe this, which I will go into in more depth later in this book. Whatever the case, she said it best here:

 Enthusiasm is common. Endurance is rare. (p. 68)

It may go without saying that passion—a strong interest in something—with no actions or behaviours that represent progress toward that thing, is not worth the paper it's written on. I think back to when I was 15 years old, proclaiming to anyone who would listen that I was going to be a millionaire by the time I was 25 years old. It turns out that talk regarding one's alleged passion is cheap. Without a path or goals, without the steps of action to take me, well, anywhere, that proclamation died a painless death.

I was guilty of what psychologist Gabriele Oettingen (1996) termed "positive fantasising"—indulging in visions of that positive future I had in mind without bothering to figure out how to get there. Other roadblocks to effective perseverance include the tendency to have lots of goals that are not unified toward that passionately held outcome. People who commit this error confuse being busy with being productive. In the case of grit, one's passion acts like a compass, impelling action that actually moves you closer to your desired destination.

I have no argument with grit. As mentioned, I was happily shocked to discover just how gritty I was (as measured by Duckworth's self-assessment tool in *Grit*). This makes me wonder if it's a feature of gritty people that we don't ever presume we actually are gritty. I can imagine the knee-jerk reaction of those who are in pursuit of lofty long-term goals to be a big "Not me!" I know personally that I'm more inclined to notice those times when my fortitude and resolve desert me. I do know that I am less inclined than when I was younger to get my knickers in a twist about my failures and to just get on with it. Whatever the case, grit has served me well, and I salute Angela Duckworth's efforts to capture this phenomenon and help us understand this aspect underpinning the psychology of achievement.

If you want to work smarter or live better, and wonder about how to do that, learning to be gritty can be a game-changer. At the same time, it's no panacea. In the rest of this book, I will be coming at grit from the other end of things to explore how and when our environments and our personalities can conspire to render our gritty efforts less effective and, at times, counterproductive. I will also share some tools I have taught performers to augment their grit and increase their effectiveness no matter the circumstance.

Coming up next in Chapter 2, the journey to the other end of the spectrum starts. I take a look at how and when grit may not be our best servant—those times when, in fact, grit may *not* be enough.

KEY TAKEAWAYS

✓ While we think and say we value effort and people who try hard, we are biased to value natural talent over effort.

✓ Behind every great talent is generally a hell of a lot of effort that we just don't see, so we don't know to value it.

✓ In fact, effort counts *twice:* Talent × Effort = Skill; Skill × Effort = Achievement.

✓ Consistent, concerted effort over time builds talent. Those who effort in this way eventually outperform the unindustrious but gifted performer.

✓ Grit = Passion + Perseverance. It's about what you care about + the enduring effort you make over time.

✓ At the same time, grit is no panacea, and like any other capability or quality, can be overindexed or overused.

2   THE DOWNSIDE OF GRIT

People in the elite sport world are almost always hooked by my book's title, *When Grit Is Not Enough*. "Wait, there may be more to it than grit?" they ask. "What do you mean?" It's as if I questioned some entry-level dogma. Yet, when I ask athletes or coaches to talk about a time when they were too gritty or overused it, I will—not always, but regularly enough—get a knowing chuckle and a wry story about some ill-considered gritty effort that did not end well.

Let's be clear, though. There are plenty of times when grit may be, indeed, all you need: when you have enough talent and a willingness to make the sustained effort, and the long-term vision for where you are headed is stable and durable. Not to make any of that sound easy—it is not. The ability to maintain enduring effort and withstand failure, the dips in motivation, and the rest of it is nothing to be quibbled with.

The intuitive understanding that grit is a useful quality is not universal by any stretch. In my work forays outside elite sport and other high-performance domains, for example, the drop in personal levels of grit is noticeable if not downright obvious. If you have not experienced truly sustained hard effort, don't know what it looks like, or are not surrounded by others who do, how would you know?

When Grit's in the Water

No doubt this is why people like Angela Duckworth are so interested in how to develop this concept, especially in kids, as this combination of capabilities can and does take people to places that they might not otherwise go. But it wasn't until I consciously thought about it that the environmental discrepancy became so apparent to me. In my career as a sport psychologist for elite sport, I have been marinating in a world awash in grit. It reminds me of the joke that celebrated author David Foster Wallace (2005) made famous in a college commencement speech:

> There are two young fish swimming along who happen to meet an older fish. The older fish nods at them and says, "Morning, boys. How's the water?" The two young fish swim on for a bit, and then eventually one of them looks over at the other and asks, "What the hell is water?"

When the domain one swims in requires long bouts of hard effort and pain, grit isn't just *in* the water; it *is* the water. It is from this vantage point—a world where high levels of passion, perseverance, and hard effort are so ubiquitous that having them just gets you a ticket to the cheap seats—that the likelihood of overdoing it starts to make sense. If everyone around you is acting this way, and if they are recognised and rewarded for their efforts, it can make a lot of sense to think, "If a little is good, shouldn't more be better?"

Grit Overdone: Rigidity and Myopia

I have noticed two ways in which athletes and coaches start to overindex on their grit. The first pertains to a lack of flexibility in response to circumstance—when circumstances change and the individual fails to adapt. Take the case in point of 2020, when the global pandemic upended sport conventional wisdom in the most profound way since World War II. Elite sport is nothing if not planned out to the nth degree. It functions on a predictable, global event schedule, on scripted training programs, on multidisciplinary teams, and world-class facility access. The Covid pandemic scattered those structures and plans to the wind. Not only were competitions including the Olympics postponed, but teams were disbanded and individuals sent to hunker down in individual isolation. Training camps were scheduled, delayed, scheduled, and delayed again. So plans were not only changed but often left in long-term limbo. If you don't even know where you are headed, how can you begin to recraft your passion, much less persevere toward it in any coherent way?

Athletes and coaches responded in a variety of ways to this chronic uncertainty—not all well. Coping in this changed reality required, for some, quick acquisition of a new and different set of skills, as well as the perspective and insight to see this as an opportunity—to learn new ways to work—rather than merely a threat—"I'm unable to do things my preferred way." Reliance on grit in this situation was counterproductive when it meant blind adherence to what used to work.

The second way that grit can fail is in the form of a personal myopia. Having found and seemingly perfected their gritty processes, people in this context overfocus on their gritty efforts to their own detriment.

Scott Brennan, 2008 Olympic rowing double sculls gold medallist, is hands-down one of the grittiest humans I know. His mind arced to grit at an early age. He described the first time he realised that a gritty mindset would be a desirable thing, at the tender age of 11.

> I was playing basketball, and I absolutely stacked it on the bitumen, and I was just in shorts and a T-shirt. And just something was different that time, as in before that point, if I'd lost a lot of skin, I probably would have cried and been really upset. But this time, I was like, "Yes, I'm bleeding; yes, that really hurts; but what am I actually afraid of? Like, what's the problem? Yes, it really hurts, but it's not going to hurt forever." And at the time I remember being really struck by the idea that "Yeah, I'm really different now. Something's changed." I didn't know what it was. And it wasn't a negative or a positive, but just like, "Oh, I don't cry anymore." That comes back to the understanding "What am I really afraid of here?"

Layered onto this natural proclivity for self-awareness, Scott also shared how experience also intervened in term

of his life-altering story about contracting septic arthritis as
a teenager.

*My understanding of physical pain was completely recalibrated
at the age of 16. At the time I had fallen ill with a relatively mild
pneumonia that was altogether unremarkable until I later began
to develop an ache deep in my right lower back/hip region.*

*I thought it was a strained muscle, but it was progressing to the
point I was now unable to sit still in class. I was unaware that bac-
teria had invaded the joint and were beginning to cause damage
to the tissues there. Within 48 hours, the infection was running
rampant and destroying the joint. I was critically unwell, floridly
delirious, and raving with pain.*

*To anyone with sacro-iliac joint issues who knows how integral
that joint is to the physical mechanics of coughing (let alone
basic movements like rolling over in bed), to be suffering a con-
current pneumonia when struck down by an already exceedingly
rare condition seemed impossibly cruel luck.*

*It has been over 20 years since that time, but I certainly don't
need to close my eyes to be able to recall exactly what it was
like. I lay utterly still for days on end, too scared to move should
the inflamed joint edges shear across each other in the process.
Each time I coughed, reality would warp in a crystalline shatter-
ing of white searing pain that either rendered me briefly uncon-
scious or otherwise left me so deeply convinced I had ceased to*

exist that I began to question my sanity and whether or not I had actually already died.

I have been told on occasion that I am tough, that I have a "high pain threshold," but I don't believe that at all. I feel pain no more or less than anyone else with a normally functioning nervous system. What I have is a different perspective—a hideous under-standing of what pain can be and **how much worse it can get before you hit a ceiling where nothing else exists**, and I never, ever, want to go back there. I don't believe I am strong enough to survive it a second time.

While I wouldn't wish it on my worst enemy, the silver lining to it all is that kind of altered perspective can be useful in professional sport. People like to use numbers out of 10 to rate pain, so if the septic arthritis was my 10/10, then in comparison, perhaps I've touched a 3 a few other times in my life with particularly painful injuries or surgeries. But it's not about the physical pain itself at all. Much like with the basketball incident as a child, it was an understanding of the emotional meaning that lies behind noxious stimuli my brain was receiving.

The exertional discomfort of sport was a life-affirming discom-fort, an appropriate sensation that I had complete control over and that I could make stop at any time of my choosing. It was the true antithesis of what I had suffered through, alone at night in that hospital. I believe it was why I felt my most alive any time I was in the closing stages of a tightly fought international race, revelling in the gloriously voluntary discomfort—precisely at the *point where many others started to question "Why?" I was just finding myself shouting, "We ain't dead yet!"*

I don't know about you, but this story boggled my mind. Though Scott was his characteristic matter-of-fact self in telling it, it is hard to imagine, much less live through, this tale. So we have an athlete who had both a natural bent toward a "quiet" mindset when it came to pain, but who also barely survived a pain experience so exquisite, it forever recalibrated his understanding of the upper limits of pain, thereby rendering anything less—including the pain of exertion in the last 200 meters of an Olympic rowing final—as not only doable but something worth celebrating.

Scott's unique mindset was such that he could see through mental errors and the stories his mind would tell under extreme pain and exertion, first in himself, then in terms of how others, even his opponents, were likely to be thinking. He was not, by his own admission, the most mentally tough or the most gifted athlete, but he had a natural—and learned—bent toward grit in how he approached his rowing training and competition. In our conversations, he would profess puzzlement at how other rowers would complain or struggle, when to his mind, it was simply their mental approach that was wanting.

An unfortunate string of injuries in the run-up to the 2012 Olympics scuttled the medal hopes of Scott and his doubles partner, David Crawshay (they eventually finished in eighth place) and plunged Scott into a dark time as he sought to rehabilitate a seemingly undiagnosable back problem. He returned to work with me during that time, when doctors suggested that his injury might be more psychological than physical. We found no evidence of that or of any particular trauma, just a maddeningly frustrating and stubborn injury. His search for a solution took him to Canada and some less conventional therapies. Scott described the arc his life took at that point—literally years of eight-hour-per-day rehabilitation in the hope of returning to the elite rowing ranks in time for the 2016 Olympics:

> This nebulous thing of my injury was impacting everything in my life. That was all there was. I got to the point where I was hating what I was doing. I hated it. But this promise it would maybe get better . . . by then all the passion had been ground out of me so the only reason why I was still going was that I wasn't going to give in. I was a gritty person and gritty people don't give in. I would push and push and just get more miserable.
>
> Until one day, it was like, "If I give up, why is that a bad thing?" I can look back at what I have done and understand that it's all I could have done. How many other people would have done that? "How good do you need to be, mate? Is this about your ego? Are you worried what they will think? If I am not happy, then why am I here?"
>
> I hadn't really thought about it: that's just who I am and I am going to do it. Once I actually stepped back and said, "This much is my ego, this much is me, this is what other people have invested . . ." and defined it all out, the next morning I woke up and said, "I'm retiring." Bang. It was, like, so obvious.

Flipping Grit's Downside for Better Results

If these examples resonate at all for you—chronic inflexibility or a too-laser-like focus that has lost perspective—this book can help. You will learn about what you can do to make your grit more fit for purpose and adaptable to change, uncertainty, and the vicissitudes of life.

I used to think that Covid would go away and that there would no longer be the kind of global disruption that tests grit as it has, but I don't think that anymore. First, I don't think we will soon, if ever, return to our pre-Covid world. This pandemic is too wily and durable.

Second, and as important, the tools I share in this book are win-win-win, pandemic or no. Win #1: They can be added to your grit repertoire and will augment your best efforts. Win #2: They will allow you to more quickly and intelligently pivot in response to circumstance. Win #3: Layering these skills onto what you already have going will make your life happier and more satisfying.

While Chapters 1 and 2 have made the case for and against grit, from here we start the grit-enhancing insight and skill-building journey. Coming next, Chapter 3 lays out the case for how we humans developed our aversion to change and uncertainty, as well as why we tend to go straight to the worst-case scenario. Understanding this landscape is important as we contemplate how to override our instincts when necessary.

KEY TAKEAWAYS

✓ The idea and practice of being gritty is inherent in some, but not all environments.

✓ For those who lack grit, learning about and applying oneself to developing this capability can be very useful. Read the book *Grit*.

✓ Where grit is inherent in a culture—like sport—it's seductive to think that if a little grit is good, more must be better. And that can be the road to grit ruin.

✓ We overdo it on grit in two ways: when we are so rigid in our approach that we fail to flex when circumstances change, and when our myopic self-focus overwhelms our ability to "see the big picture" and adjust accordingly.

✓ The rest of this book is about how to address the urge to overindex on grit and learn alternative ways to operate that can increase your mental flexibility and make performance easier.

PART II
INTRODUCTION TO MINDSET

There's a paradox for us humans when we try to navigate times of uncertainty. Not only are we discomfited when we don't know what to expect, but our brains are hard-wired to want the opposite: predictability and comfort. *If I can predict the future and if I'm smart about it, I can plan for it and maximise my chances for success.* Of course, even when that's the case, when we know what will happen (say, for example, in any other Olympic year, we all know when it's coming and what the rules of engagement are), we can still fall short of maxing out our preparation; but at least this kind of certainty provides explanations for success or failure in an endeavour.

In times of uncertainty, it's as if we are hiking along a mountain ridge, aiming for the yonder peak, but our immediate environment as well as the peak is blanketed in fog. We try to see where we are going, but the fog is too thick. We can't see where we are going and worry about our footing. At this point, fear may set in, paralysing us, or we become angry, cursing the fog for standing between us and our goal. We may wonder if we will ever get to where we want to go or, worse, get wound up in "what if?" thoughts of potential injury, hypothermia, or even death.

Image by Pexels from Pixabay

Living in times of chronic uncertainty can feel like this sometimes. At the start of the pandemic, for example, no one could predict with any accuracy what was going to happen in six months. *Will enough people have been vaccinated? Will the vaccines be effective? Will international borders open up without testing and quarantine requirements? Will the next Olympics happen on time . . . or at all?*

It turns out that there's another way to approach this scenario.

Even in the densest fog, there may be the occasional wind-driven swirls and eddies that give us glimpses of what's ahead. At the same time, if we look straight down at our hiking boots and what's in our immediate surroundings, we can usually make out the terrain at least a few yards ahead. By focusing on what we can see and attending to our footing, we can move a few feet forward . . . and repeat the process. We take a few careful steps and see where they lead us. We also keep in mind the pragmatic reality that no fog lasts forever.

We work to perceive reality as it is in front of and around us. I say that we "work" on this because it is not our preferred or even instinctive way to orient. Our minds want to worry about what might happen next.

Instead, we can learn to persist in focusing on the immediate situation rather than giving in to thoughts of how we want it to be or how we wish it were different. We can focus on what's around us right now and do the best we can with that. And after we move forward through this scenario, another experience and situation will present itself and we will deal with that as it comes.

Sometimes we might be able to plan effectively for a few or even a hundred feet at a time; sometimes not. But it's in the moving forward as the fog allows where progress—and learning—happen. This mindset saves us precious energy for the task at hand as well as for those tasks still to come.

The sceptic might say something like, "But what if you head off the wrong way?" Of course there's a chance for a worse outcome, but then that reality will present itself, and a new, tweaked course can be determined.

Rather than fighting the foggy reality—straining our eyeballs trying to see that peak and railing against the impenetrable fog—we accept its obscurity with a sense of relative calm and neutrality, allowing it to be no more or less than it actually is. This acceptance can give us the mental space to make better, more considered decisions.

This mindset shift can grate for those athletes and coaches used to having predictability, control, and action. I am reminded of a colleague I worked with during the 2008 Beijing

Olympics. There, the Olympic Park containing many different venues was especially sprawling and directions were confusing. We would start off somewhere and be unsure of our direction, which only made my colleague speed up. When asked about his haste, what was his invariable response? "At least we're getting *somewhere*!" I'll give him points for comic relief even though these efforts often did more harm than good in terms of getting us to our destination, much less on time.

Often, our knee-jerk reaction to the idea of "acceptance" is one of fear or even contempt. Acceptance of the situation as it is can be mistaken for being too soft or passive. "If I just let this happen to me, aren't I just giving up? Rolling over and taking it? Won't I lose my edge?" Like my colleague in Beijing, inaction, or even stopping to go into a building to get oriented or ask for directions, was just not "action-y" enough. The mistake was in assuming that *any* action was better than none. Some actions are, in the end, better not undertaken, or could at least benefit from some course corrections along the way.

I'd argue that learning the skills of interpreting our reality as accurately and dispassionately as possible and *accepting* what's on offer as quickly as possible gives us *more* power, not less. When we can read the situation and accept it for what it is, we can then make better, more considered decisions, saving our energy for what matters right now.

In an effort to clear the fog, the chapters in Section 2 lay the foundation for developing the mindset that can help turbocharge your grit.

- Chapter 3, "How We Evolved to Respond to Uncertainty," takes a deep(ish) dive into our evolutionary history with an eye for helping us understand some of our more annoying propensities and why we react as we do. We come by some of our foibles—our tendency toward hypervigilance and worry—honestly.

- Chapter 4, "Being Present," showcases the power of mindfulness, particularly in times of uncertainty, to help steer us away from the worst tendencies of our brains and minds toward worry and hypervigilant scanning.

- Chapter 5, "Awareness, Acceptance, Action," dips into the orientation toward uncertainty that performance psychologists suggest lies at the heart of thriving.

- Chapter 6, "Making Friends with Yourself," looks at the resilience-protecting qualities of compassion and self-compassion as buffers against stress, failure, and uncertainty.

3 HOW WE EVOLVED TO RESPOND TO UNCERTAINTY

Human beings do not handle uncertainty well. It can make us uncomfortable, infuriated, or anxious by turns. Some of the reactivity we experience in the face of uncertainty is of our own making, but a lot of our reactions are literally hard-wired, baked in over the millennia of human existence.

Image by Hambone Publishing

Consider this scenario from tens of thousands of years ago. Two cave people are standing, looking out over the savanna.

One caveman—we'll call him Ed—is a happy-go-lucky optimist. The other—let's call her Sue—is a cynical pessimist. As they gaze at the grassy plain before them, a breeze can be seen to be creating ripples through the grass.

Every time a big ripple comes through, Sue gives a start and runs away from the perceived threat: perhaps a sabre-toothed tiger? Ed, on the other hand, stays put, enjoying the lovely tableau while chuckling at Sue's fright. This happens time and time again, with Ed feeling quite sorry for Sue's angst—until that time when, as fate would have it, the ripple in the grass is not caused by the breeze, but by the stalking tiger that pounces on poor Ed and enjoys a tasty lunch.

The moral of this story? If you wanted to survive in a world filled with unpredictable threat, your probabilities went up if you were a pessimist like Sue, always scanning for and running away from the slightest whiff of perceived threat. And with that greater chance of surviving longer, pessimists were more likely to pass on their genes to the next generation, and the one after that, the one after that, and so on—in effect, filtering out over thousands of years the likelihood of an optimistic, happy-go-lucky nature and selecting for hypervigilance and a pessimistic nature that presumed, and ran from, the worst-case scenario.

This story illustrates a fundamental truth about evolution: we have not evolved to be happy, necessarily; rather, we have evolved to survive.

Why is this story important for us in sport in the face of change and uncertainty? Understanding that our tendencies toward feeling anxious and assuming the worst-case scenario are largely a function of instinct rather than conscious choice should be a relief to those of us who have questioned our tendencies or castigated ourselves for our anxiety, sense of weakness, frustration, or other seemingly irrational responses. This is not to say that we are powerless to do anything about our reactions, but that we come by those often knee-jerk reactions honestly. It's bad enough that life hands us uncertainty and we suffer as a result of it. It's profoundly worse—not to mention destructive and unnecessary—when we label our instinctive reactions as wrong or shameful.

That last paragraph was meant to be a comfort for those of us who suffer from this kind of doomsday thinking; but knowing why we are the way we are doesn't do much to ease our suffering now. I imagine that many of us would gladly give away our chronic anxieties for an easier approach to life's uncertainties.

Hang in there. Just because that's the way your brain evolved does not mean those habits have to stay that way for the motivated learner. Motivated learners? The rest of this book is for you.

Unpacking the Modern Brain from Old to New

The human brain evolved from back to front, as shown in Figure 3.1.

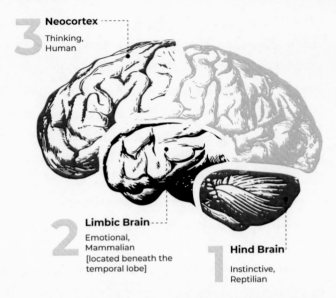

Figure 3.1. How the Human Brain Evolved: Instinctive, Emotional, Thinking
Image by StarGladVintage on Pixabay

First to evolve was our hind brain, shown in Figure 3.1 as number 1. This part of our brain sits at the top of our spinal cord and is what we share with all other species on the planet. Here is where our autonomic functioning—activities such as breathing, heart rate, and blood pressure regulation—is controlled without our conscious awareness.

Next to evolve was our limbic brain, shown in the figure as number 2, the part of our brain responsible for functions such as memory and, most notably for our purposes, our emotions. This order of development is important to understand and one of the reasons we are so skilled at threat detection. Early on, we needed mechanisms to keep us safe from all the threats of the early human world, including predators, other humans, and nature itself. Emotions were the answer, and they developed as triggers for the "4 F" threat-response behaviours: fight, flight, freeze, and (no joke, this was right out of my college neurobiology textbook) making love.

To this day, we have a constellation of emotion-behaviour patterns we instinctively default to in response to threat. Fleeing and freezing are the body's instinctive responses to fear. Fighting is triggered by anger, and making love is—at least sometimes—an antidote to stress.

This order of events is understandable if we accept that the purpose of emotions was and is to keep us safe from threat. Imagine that you are driving along a road and a car suddenly drifts into your lane going the other way. You don't have to think much about your reaction—your fear triggers your instinctive turn of the steering wheel and your urge to jam on the brake to avert oncoming disaster. It is only after you have stopped the car, panting due to delayed-onset physiological stress response, that you think, "What the hell just happened?" Not only do our brains process emotions first, but our brains are much faster at processing emotions than thoughts.

Our most recent brain evolution is also what separates us from the rest of the species on the planet. That part of the brain is the neocortex (number 3 in Figure 3.1), which governs our thinking and decision-making processes. We are the only species able to think about our thinking. That is, we can become aware not only of the fact that we *are* thinking, but of the quality and usefulness of any given thought. Here, too, is where we can think forward and backward in time, presumably to learn more effectively and efficiently from the past and better plan for the future.

Behavioural Implications of the Brain's Evolution

Taken in context, this order of evolutionary events makes sense. Our hind brain operates on constant auto-pilot, running the autonomic-functioning show and keeping us alive, at times seemingly despite ourselves. Before we could think or communicate, the limbic system's emotions evolved to protect us from the many threats we faced over the millennia. More recently, we developed, with the addition of the neocortex, our capacity for thought, which separates us from all other species and could be said in some ways to define the human race and its domination of all other forms of life, and the planet itself.

This evolutionary order of business has meant some unanticipated bumps for humans. The fact that the brain processes emotions before thoughts can create problems for us, especially under conditions of high stress or threat. Our limbic-system responses to threat were designed in a time when the threats around us could kill or maim us. Those immediate and serious threats called for a sudden marshalling of our human resources to make that quick and dirty escape. Post threat, our system would rapidly return to equilibrium so we could recover in time to deal with the next threat.

One modern-day issue with this system is that most (but not all) of our 21st century threats are not seeking to kill us. The threats we face are often more existential and lack actual substance; but make no mistake, they are perceived as credible threats to our egos, our status, our ambitions, and/or our future.

Moreover, so many of today's threats are ongoing, posing risks to our ability to withstand their effects given that our internal threat detection and avoidance systems were not built for things like chronic angst and prolonged high stress. Neuroscientist Judson Brewer (2021), in his book *Unwinding Anxiety: Train Your Brain to Heal Your Mind,* suggests that we can learn something from zebras and dogs that, after surviving a stressful situation, jump and kick or shake their bodies in a literal effort to discharge the excess energy associated with that "I almost died" adrenaline surge. His advice is that we humans should do likewise and, rather than just talking about a stressful situation, consider adding in exercise or even dancing, to "shake it off."

The bottom line here is that we need better stress management and adrenaline-busting strategies. Many of today's chronic health conditions are a result of our system's inability to properly cope with our daily and ongoing stressors.

Related to this is that, when we are faced with sudden stress or threat, our thinking brains can go off-line entirely, resulting in what psychologist and author Daniel Goleman (1995), in his book *Emotional Intelligence,* calls the Limbic Hijack. That is, when the threat overwhelms our thinking abilities, our brain devolves to that more primitive but also more practiced threat-detection and coping system. Brain imaging suggests that the limbic networks are just that much more efficient than our prefrontal "thinking" networks; and when instant action is perceived to be required, the limbic system takes over.

While the threat is addressed quickly in these hijack

situations, our more primitive strategies and solutions are not always ideal responses for the stressful situation. Road rage is an example of our primitive anger reactions running amok, often creating a worse situation for the person who is so overcome. Sian Beilock (2010), in her book *Choke*, points out that it is the limbic hijack that is so often the cause of athletes seeming to lose the ability to execute even simple, well-rehearsed skills in the face of high-pressure situations in sport.

The Good News

While all of these brain-processing limitations may be biologically true, the excellent news is that, through our ability to think and learn, thanks to our neocortex, we can actually offset our biological limitations in this space. This understanding forms the basis for the rest of this section of the book. I will be sharing different ways to approach reality and develop a different, more helpful relationship with both our thoughts as well as our emotions, in the interest of coping more effectively through times of change and uncertainty.

We start that journey in the next chapter with an understanding of why "being present" more often is so important for our well-being, how it can actually help us coexist in more harmony with our emotions as well as our thoughts, and how it can also improve our performance.

KEY TAKEAWAYS

✓ Humans do not handle uncertainty well. Our brains are, through evolution, hard-wired for threat. As a result, we reflexively overfocus on the negative possibilities that uncertainty foreshadows rather than on the opportunities.

✓ Moreover, our natural threat detection and reaction processes can be likened to "blunt instruments" rather than easily scaled to the actual threat that exists in the moment.

✓ Adding to this overkill issue is the fact that most threats we face in the 21st century are not going to kill us. But nevertheless, our brains tend to overreact as if death is in the offing, rendering us less effective just when we need to be the opposite.

✓ While the older parts of our brain (hind brain and limbic brain) maintain this threat focus, the good news is that the newer parts of our brain (neocortex) can be trained to mitigate this tendency.

✓ We are unique among all the species on the planet in that we can think about our thinking. This "meta-awareness" can be developed to help us counteract our more primitive ways of operating in response to 21st century threats.

4   BEING PRESENT

Talk to any elite athlete and they will tell you that, when they are playing at their best, they are . . . right here. In the moment. Sometimes they are even in flow, that elusive mind state where they are fully immersed in and intensely focused on the activity, time seems to slow down, and they are enjoying every minute. This state could be considered the mental "holy grail" of sport, as it neatly sidesteps so many common mental pitfalls elite athletes experience yet can be maddeningly elusive.

We have all heard of this idea—to "be here now"—to the point that we stop listening to its inherent wisdom. The present moment's power is that it's the only moment we have any influence over. We can't rewrite the past, and the future has yet to be written. This concept is easy to understand in a performance domain like sport, where athletes' actions are so directly tied to the quality of whatever behaviour or technique they are executing in a given moment.

Too often, athletes who allow their attention to get stuck on a past mistake are in no position to make the best decision the next instant they must perform and are in a position of "right now" influence. Instead, too much emphasis is placed on "making up for the past mistake" and not enough on what needs to be done now, often leading to yet another mistake or miscue. Equally, the annals of sport are filled with stories of athletes who, when ahead in the score or the race, "let up" by allowing their attention to drift forward into the future—to the anticipated glory of the finish—and then are overcome or passed by a hungrier competitor.

To be fair, the phrase "be here now" implies that we are somewhere else and that we should stop doing that. But what does that really mean?

Our Time-Travelling Tendencies

Being here, being present, is a mental game, for sure. Our bodies can't be anywhere *but* here. The thing is, we are all too often unthinking time travellers—in our minds, anyway. Without even being aware of it, the emotion-and-thinking dance that our minds are constantly engaged in propels us into the future or keeps us rooted in the past (Figure 4.1). Our fears, worries, and anxieties send our minds out ahead, scouting for threat and spinning narratives of "what if" scenarios. We worry, worry, worry about the big competition or upcoming selections, watching the situation approach us in time. Suddenly the event is upon us—we get through it, succeed, or fail—and as suddenly, that situation has been relegated to the past. As if by magic, we stop worrying about that situation, too busy casting ahead again for the next anxiety-provoking thing.

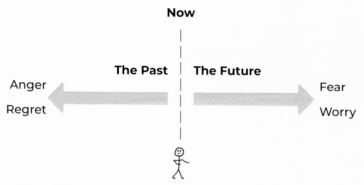

Figure 4.1. Our Bodies Are Present, But Our Minds Can Be Anywhere

Not only do we quickly reboard the worry train, but we are less likely to take the time to reflect back on the utility of our worry after the anticipated problem event passes. Did our worries come true or not? So often, our worst-case scenario mind overestimates the risk of an event, but then it doubles down on the error by not course-correcting afterward. Our worrier tendency to favour hypervigilance over learning means that we are less likely to learn from our worry mistakes and more likely to keep on worrying.

On the other hand, emotions such as regret and anger can tend to anchor us to what has already happened. Try this mind game: Think of something that is likely to make you angry but that hasn't happened yet, an anticipated argument with a partner or teammate, perhaps. You can imagine that it would make you angry; you might even feel a tinge of irritation, but most people can't get very angry about something that hasn't yet happened. But cast into your past about an injustice you previously experienced and see how differently the emotions are carried, how much easier it is to re-experience the actual feelings of anger.

There may be times when stepping out of the present, looking back and reflecting on what just happened, is useful. Using competition as an example—say, at halftime when the coach gets her team to reflect on what worked in the first half and what will need to change to dominate the opponent in the second. But there are also other times when it is oh-so-not-helpful. When I worked with the Australian women's water polo team, we would review game video to discern when players would quite literally dunk themselves under water after a mistake. Done quickly, this tactic could have the effect of a reset button. It was when the athlete hung out under water, and you could almost sense the internal berating that was going on, that things became problematic. The angry, regretful overfocus on that mistake would lead to self-focused rumination or to over-commitment to a rash plan to "make up for it," more often than not leading to yet another mistake.

Similarly, moving one's focus from the present to the future has its uses as well. The team that has debriefed the first half of their game now has a chance to craft and mentally rehearse a second-half plan to increase the chances the proposed changes will (a) be remembered, and (b) actually work. On a more pedestrian level, without our ability to think into the future and plan out our day, we'd get little done and be late for everything.

The Power of the Present

While thinking about the past and future has its purpose, as we have noted, spending too much time in those domains can often be either unpleasant or not particularly useful—or both, especially if we are interested in our own high performance.

The present is, more often than not, where it's at. Unconvinced? Here are two exceedingly compelling reasons to think again: impact and happiness.

Impact

The present moment is the only one we can impact. The past has already been written. The future is still up for grabs. Too many athletes get caught up in focusing on either of these alternatives, to their peril, in the sense that even momentary focus on one or the other means taking your eye off the prize, which is what is on offer, right here, right now. In sport, even a momentary loss of focus on what's right in front of you can have devastating consequences.

A high-profile example comes to us from the 1988 Winter Olympic Games, where American speed skater Dan Jansen was then the reigning world sprint champion and favoured to win the 500- and 1,000-meter races. Hours before his first race, Jansen learned that his sister was dying of cancer, and then that she later died that day. Vowing to win the race in her honour, Jansen instead fell in both of his races, leaving the Olympics without a medal (Phillips, 1988).

It was impossible to focus. That's not an excuse, but it didn't go very well for me. I tried. But nobody in Calgary had ever been in that position before, so there was nobody that I could lean on for advice. I just did what I thought I should do—which we decided as a family—and that was to go out and try my best, because that's what Jane would have wanted. And I did. With having said that, I didn't have any of that physical or mental preparation that you would normally have on race day. I just figured that I would go out there and do what I always did, but my level of focus wasn't where it needed to be. And with speed skating, when your mind isn't all there it really shows. (McClellan, 2017)

In an example from my own professional life, I recall the heavily favoured wrestler who was inadvertently late for her match (she was in the bathroom when her match was called). Anyone there, including me, could see she was flustered as she ran into the venue on the third and final call. She got to the mat, the whistle to start the match blew, and she wasn't even prepared to be in position. Caught literally flat-footed, her opponent took immediate advantage and pinned her.

Happiness

What? Wait a minute—really? In 2010, researchers Matthew Killingsworth and Daniel Gilbert from Harvard discovered this simple yet profound truth in a study they called "A Wandering Mind Is an Unhappy Mind." In this study, participants were given smartphone technology that pinged them at various points of the day. In response, participants documented what they were doing, what they were thinking, and how they were feeling.

The results? First, that our attention is in the present moment less than 50 percent of the time—47 percent, to be precise. Second, we report to be happiest when we are in the present. When I speak of happiness in this context—and all contexts, really—I'm not talking about euphoria or joy, necessarily. While we may associate happiness with these peak experiences, happiness comes in less dramatic forms as well. It can manifest as the simple sense of contentment when you look outside your window at your garden or take the moment to appreciate the face of your friend. The point is that often the present is at least pleasant, but we fail to take notice, much less enjoy, even that.

Recall also that many of the emotions that tend to take us away from the present are, well, less pleasant. I don't know about you, but if I had my choice between worrying about some future event, ruminating angrily about some past injustice, and present-moment calm or casual interest in my surroundings, I know what I'd choose.

The point is to recognize that we do, in the end, have a choice on where we focus our attention. We just have to remember to do so.

Why Being Present Is So Hard

So, if the present moment is all that special, why aren't we able to "be here now" more often? First, we have been conditioned to devalue "just" being in the present. The sheer speed of life and the number of tasks being thrown at us makes the idea of multitasking sound brilliant; however, not only is this strategy not possible, but we are literally shortening our attentional lifespan (Madore & Wagner, 2019). When we multitask, we are not efficiently getting two (or three or four) things done at once. Rather, our brains are swiftly shifting back and forth from one task requirement to another. Not only is this very tiring for the brain, but our effectiveness at any one of the tasks we are performing goes down by as much as 40 percent (Rubenstein et al., 2001).

Second, there can be a certain mundanity to the present moment that belies its importance in our lives and to our happiness and well-being (much less our performance!). Why focus on what's right here when our smartphones and social media provide so much more stimulating content? We are losing our natural ability to be engaged with what I call "small *h*" happiness activities, or enjoying the small details inherent in this moment. And this is how mindless habits are born. I can be as shocked as anyone by the ease with which, when I have a spare moment in my day, my phone appears in my hand. I have had to work diligently for some time to learn to resist the temptation for stimulation. As I type this sentence, I take the time to look out my window at a beautiful sunny day, with the breezes swaying the trees in the yard. Sure, it's not all *that* exciting, but it is colourful and even soothing. Renowned meditation teacher Joseph Goldstein has said that "boredom means you're just not paying attention enough," which speaks to this phenomenon.

The third thief of our present-moment attention is the aforementioned tendency of our more primal emotions like anxiety, worry, anger, and regret to yank us right out of the present into our hypervigilant futures or ruminative pasts.

And finally, it's our own bias toward *doing* over *being*. Athletes, coaches, and performers alike seem to have almost a built-in bias against just sitting with what goes on in their heads. At the very least, it can sometimes be seen as a waste of time and self-indulgent. Moreover, there's research evidence that backs the notion that we don't naturally enjoy being alone with the goings-on in our own minds. Social psychologist Tim Wilson and his colleagues from the University of Virginia conducted a series of studies in which participants were instructed to spend periods of time alone with their thoughts, both in the laboratory and in their own homes. In both conditions, a surprising 50 percent of participants reported their experiences as significantly negative. In the final "thinking" condition, participants were given access to a machine that delivered, upon demand, a slightly painful but not debilitating shock. Despite all participants previously saying that they would pay money to avoid being shocked, a surprising 67 percent of men and 25 percent of women voluntarily inflicted shocks upon themselves rather than just sitting quietly and thinking (Wilson et al., 2014).

So now that we have an understanding of the importance of the present and why it's harder than we'd think to get and stay here, how can we make the present moment more palatable? The next chapter, "Awareness, Acceptance, Action," provides some ways to cultivate the ability to remain in the present and maybe even do so more happily.

KEY TAKEAWAYS

✓ The present moment is important because it is the only moment in time we can influence. The past has already been written and the future has yet to unfold.

✓ While our bodies and our senses are always in the present, our minds are expert time travellers, roaming back to our past and forward into our future at will.

✓ Our emotions are often the triggers for this mental time travel. Fear, anxiety, and worry send us off into the future, while emotions like anger and regret take us back into the past.

✓ Not all time travel is bad; we need a future focus to plan effectively, and reflecting on the past can be useful for learning.

✓ The power of the present moment is twofold: first, it's the only moment we can influence, and second, science suggests that we are happiest when we are more fully inhabiting the present.

✓ Being present for any amount of time, however, is harder than it looks. Our increasing need for constant stimulation (think social media, the sheer number of new inputs, and our addiction to technology) is undermining our ability to be present very long. Moreover, we are conditioned to dislike "just" being in the present.

5 AWARENESS, ACCEPTANCE, ACTION

The cycle of positive thought we want to develop is the triple-A combo of awareness, acceptance, and action. The "Awareness, Acceptance, Action" sequence (Figure 5.1) can be a game-changer, smoothing out our reactivity and allowing for more ease and smarter actions. This process is especially important in times of change and uncertainty, but it's useful whatever the circumstances.

Let's start by unpacking the concept of awareness.

Becoming Aware

How aware are you of how you are feeling, what you are thinking, and what is actually happening right now? Moreover, are you able to know that you are feeling and thinking without necessarily getting lost in either? As was discussed in Chapter 3, we are the only species on Earth that can figuratively "step back" and become aware of our thinking and emotional states, but just because we *can* doesn't mean we *do*— often enough or sometimes at all.

Figure 5.1. The "Awareness, Acceptance, Action" Sequence

Tasha Eurich, author of the book *Insight*, describes self-awareness in terms of how we see our own values, passions, and aspirations fitting with our environment, our reactions (including thoughts, feelings, behaviours, strengths, and weaknesses), and their impact on others. Interestingly, while

85 percent of us think that we are great at this, only 15 percent of us actually are (Eurich, 2018).

The reasons for this, as identified in Eurich's research, are intriguing and run counter to conventional wisdom. First is that our expertise and experience can often function to degrade the quality of our self-awareness. Our tendency to rely on and gain confidence from within the comfortable confines of our own expertise can take us farther away from the kind of open questioning and accurate understanding of reality we had as beginners. Moreover, the farther we move up the chain of command in any organization, the less likely we are to encounter people willing to challenge our notions of reality.

The second counterintuitive finding is that simple introspection does not lead as often as we would think toward greater self-awareness. This is due to some common mistakes we make in our attempts to understand what is happening to us. It turns out that introspection by using *why* questions, while common, is largely ineffective. "Why doesn't Coach like me?" is an understandable question but not one likely to lead to useful answers since our minds tend to fill the gaps with guesses. Moreover, *why* questions can tend to take us down a path of unhelpful, ruminative thinking that just accentuates negative feelings and reactions.

Developing and regularly engaging in healthy self-awareness is possible, easier than you might think, and a counterweight to these less effective thinking habits. Rather than thinking that it's about figuring yourself out by asking those pesky *why* questions, know that this is simply about self-observation, noticing what's happening without feeling any need to change, fix, or even make sense of it.

The key here is to resist the very natural urge to judge whatever is happening, while periodically dropping in the simple question "Am I aware?" as a way to build out that sense of awareness over time, and then seeing what comes up. It could be the realisation that lots of thinking is happening, or that emotions are being felt, or that your nose itches. Once you start noticing, it can become quickly apparent that there's a heck of a lot going on. Deepening this more accurate and non-judgmental awareness of our current internal (and external) reality provides an important foundation of self-knowledge that can't help but better inform our reactions and decisions.

Accepting Reality

Right now, it's like this. I first learned this piece of wisdom from Jay Michaelson, meditation teacher and author, who learned it from *his* meditation teacher (see the *10 Percent Happier* app for the original talk of the same name). I like this wording better than the more flippant "it is what it is," but the meanings are similar. Feelings of uncertainty or pondering an uncertain future can feel icky, uncomfortable, and at times scary; dwelling on those unpleasant sensations and emotions does not serve us well. In fact, it often increases our stress and misery.

Accepting reality is when we can observe a situation—even one we don't like (such as the fog bank described in the Section 2 intro) that prohibits us from seeing our ultimate destination or another Covid-19 shut-down—for what it actually is, rather than what our interpretation of its meaning or eventual impact is. So, what if, instead of railing against the things we don't like—traffic, an obnoxious teammate, the weather—we strive to see them as the situations they are: more cars on the road, someone with strong feelings, or, well, the weather? This approach does not change the situation itself but can have a big effect on how we react to it.

What's important here goes beyond just intellectual awareness. On the one hand, of course *right now, it's like this*. Always! How could it not be? What's the big deal? The wisdom comes from the *attitude* we bring to this statement. While we are uniquely equipped as humans to think about what is happening to us—as opposed to other species that have much more rudimentary defences against changes in the environment— our thoughts are less accurate or useful than we think. We are often caught up in wishing for things to either stay the same or to be different, which can't help but shift our perspective and colour our attitude toward reality.

Almost always, it is not reality itself that is the biggest problem, but the story *about* that reality that we tell ourselves. Consider this example:

Event reality: I was nervous, raced poorly, and did not win the heat race that would have allowed me to advance to the finals.

My story about that reality: I was really nervous before the race, imagining worst-case scenarios and doubting my abilities. Engrossed in these stories, I became overwhelmed by the pressure I felt and, forgetting my race plan, I went out way too hard *and blew up about halfway through my event. With nothing left in my tank, it was all I could do to hang on until the end of the race.*

I'm devastated and ashamed. I am hopeless and never get the big events right. Everyone will be so disappointed. How can I rock up to training or face my parents?

It takes skill, awareness, and lots of patience to separate out reality *as it is* versus how we are reacting to it. What is also interesting is how our own reactions can actually obscure the truth of reality, which can make it simultaneously worse and better than it actually is. It's easy to imagine that the judgmental story this athlete is telling—by labelling, predicting, and black-and-white thinking about what happened—is increasing their negative emotional experience of the event.

Sometimes the most powerful thing I can do with an athlete is to help them look with open eyes, yet with kindness, at what *might* happen or what actually *did* happen. Human beings typically hate to face what they don't like: the possibility of failure, the fact of loss, or even death. Yet all these things are such a part of life, and to deny them is to deny the wholeness of who we are.

Yep, you lost. Sitting with the baldness of that fact can feel excruciating, but in the end, this feeling is simply a very understandable and yes, human reaction. And, just like the weather, feelings like this come...and they go. This process should not be rushed, ignored, or fought against.

Of course, on one level, you and everyone else knows you lost. That's part of the beauty, allure, and agony of sport—the public nature of it. But knowing and accepting are two different things. Sitting with the reality of your outcome, reviewing the events that led to it, allowing the feelings (grief, disappointment, anger, or frustration) to be there *and* accepting all of it for no more or less than what it is, takes knowing to a new and wiser level.

The other insight that comes with the statement *right now, it's like this* is in the "right now" part—as in, nothing lasts forever, change is inevitable. So even though it is undeniably like this *now*, things will sooner or later change. Even the excruciating pain of loss will fade in time and perhaps even provide us with some valuable perspective. So for situations we find unpleasant, this idea may be a comfort.

But equally, as the saying goes, all good things come to an end, too. Yet how many times have we reacted as if that were a surprise and, as interesting, we experienced some anticipatory disappointment at the thought of something good ending? Think of the Sunday night "blues" we might feel at the mere thought of the weekend ending and having to go back to work on Monday.

Warning: Many high-achievers have a knee-jerk negative response to the idea of "acceptance" as seemingly unutterably passive, and so they resist the idea entirely. Don't make this mistake. Rather than seeing *acceptance* and *action* as an either-or proposition, know that they are a package deal. Too many of us action-oriented types skip or minimize the act of perceiving reality as accurately as possible—the point of acceptance—which can actually undermine the efficacy of any action we take. Accept . . . then act.

Acting Accordingly

When I am aware enough to accurately, calmly, and rationally perceive my inner and outer reality, I have *better* data from which to make decisions and judgments. When I am able to accept reality on its own terms while not taking it personally or wishing it to be different, I save emotional energy and lessen my own reactivity. These preconditions don't guarantee better actions, but they sure increase the probabilities.

Then it's a matter of deciding: to act or not to act. Consider the stressful or uncertain situations where you acted on instinct and later regretted it. Victor Frankl, scholar, Holocaust survivor, and author of the book *Man's Search for Meaning,* said it this way:

Between stimulus and response there is a space.
In that space is our power to choose our response.
In our response lies our growth and our freedom.

It's that space that can offer up the chance to pause and act more wisely, rather than auto-defaulting to what we do most often, or give in to knee-jerk reactivity, given the circumstances.

And even if the situation is such that we lack the ability to do anything useful or directly impactful, our actions in this space can become internal, in the sense that we are actively working on continued acceptance, how we can support others, or even how we can be a better version of ourselves in our local world. Science supports the notion that even small gestures such as being nice to those around us and performing small acts of kindness can be game-changers for our well-being and happiness.

In the next chapter, "Making Friends with Yourself," I unpack the counterintuitive notion that rather than being hard on ourselves for success, we really should be seeking to be kinder, and in so doing, we actually build our resilience.

KEY TAKEAWAYS

✓ We know that it's harder than it looks to return and stay in the present for any amount of time. Using the Awareness, Acceptance, Action process can help offset those natural tendencies.

✓ **Awareness** is the act of knowing what's happening in your mind without getting caught up in the happening—knowing that you're thinking, for example, without getting lost in the thoughts themselves.

✓ We are not as aware as we think. While 85 percent of us think we are self-aware, only 15 percent of us actually are. Surprising things that limit our ability to be accurately self-aware are our own expertise and experience, the ineffective ways we try to be self-aware, and our tendency to be overly judgemental about ourselves, which all act to cloud true self-awareness

✓ **Acceptance** of reality is a skill that we often have to learn, especially if our tendency is to fight it, instead. *Right now,* *it's like this* can be a useful mantra to have on hand to remind us of this thunderous, if underappreciated truth.

✓ High achievers in particular can struggle with acceptance, seeing it as a too-passive approach to life. Rather than seeing acceptance as an end to itself, remember that it's but the precursor to action. Acceptance gives us the pause to read the situation better and then take smarter action.

✓ **Acting accordingly** is the final step in the process. This can mean taking considered action in the world or managing yourself when action is not possible or called for.

6 MAKING FRIENDS WITH YOURSELF

I n the last few chapters, we explored how the brain and the mind can distort our relationship to reality and learned some ways to hack our way around these instinctive but not always helpful biases. In this chapter, we take a critical look at another relationship—the one with ourselves. Along the way, I discuss why so many of us find the very notion of self-kindness distasteful, and how ignoring this relationship can actually undermine our resilience.

First, some background and context. Angela Duckworth's research found that grit is a combination of passion and perseverance. What underpins passion? Awareness—specifically, *self-awareness*. Gritty people possess the self-awareness to recognise and own their passion. It would be damned hard to be inspired by your passion if you weren't aware you had any or didn't know what your passion actually was. I talk more about the passion part of this equation in the next section.

Perseverance, on the other hand, is all about *behaviour*. I can think all day long about my passion to make a million dollars off my business, but it's the doing of the work, over and over again, that actually increases my chances of getting there. *Rocky's* success as a cinematic franchise—and what made a generation of movie-goers fall a little in love with Sylvester Stallone's character—is all about his behavioural personification of grit.

If grit—the kind of grit that fuels *sustainable* high performance—is a stool, then self-awareness and behaviour are but two of the legs. We need another leg to keep the stool from collapsing. The third leg is our *relationship with ourselves* along the way. See Figure 6.1 for an overview of these three legs.

Self-Awareness

I can observe my thoughts and emotions without them owning me or driving me to knee-jerk decisions or reactions.

Self-Compassion

I value who I am, I celebrate my successes and commiserate on failures, and I have my own back.

Behaviour

I'm taking considered action in line with what I want.

Self-Awareness

Intentional Action

Self-Kindness

Behaviour

Self-Compassion

Resilience

Figure 6.1. The Three Legs of the Sustainable-Performance Stool

Specifically, with regard to this relationship with ourselves, I'm talking about how we *treat* ourselves. Would we describe our inner mental battles as reminiscent of fight scenes out of a *Rocky* movie? Are we hard on ourselves? Do we belittle or otherwise undermine ourselves? When we make mistakes, are we particularly harsh? Or are we able to inject a sense of friendliness or kindness into this relationship, no matter the circumstances? Are we able to and do we provide comfort to ourselves when the going is tough and we are hurting?

Going from *Rocky* to kindness in one paragraph might be making some of your heads spin, but stay with me. There is a substantial body of neuroscience research to back up the premise that this relationship—the one we have with ourselves—can make or break our resilience and therefore bolster or undermine our attempts to be gritty.

Self-Compassion: The Third Leg of the Stool

The official term for this relationship to self is *self-compassion*. But before we go there, let's first consider the meaning of *compassion*.

Compassion, if we return to its Latin roots, translates to the phrase "to suffer with." This is the idea that, when we see someone else suffering, we are naturally drawn, even evolutionarily primed, to provide gestures or words of kindness and support to that person. Compassion is known to social scientists as one element of our suite of prosocial emotions—along with empathy and even guilt—emotions that serve to keep us in community by, for example, drawing us together or prompting us to make amends when we have done something wrong.

Compassion might be expressed in words, a smile, a touch,

or a hug. Even if we can't solve the problem causing someone else's suffering, we can be there, suffering with them, which in and of itself can provide significant value. Consider the old chestnut "A burden shared is a burden halved" and recall a time when someone reached out to share your burden when you were suffering. How did that feel?

Standing with Others

In times of uncertainty and change, no "right mindset" is complete without attention paid to how we treat others (as well as ourselves), especially if they—or we—are struggling. Moreover, the idea of raising our game in this regard is good at any point and for all seasons, but especially for athletes and coaches in the crucible of high performance.

Elite sport is an environment where, if we are doing things right, we are often living on the cusp of failure. Otherwise, how would coaches and athletes know where the current performance limits are? Athletes who are working to master technique will not always get it right. Coaches rely on expertise, experience, and their intuition to work out best-fit training regimes, and this kind of innovation never goes perfectly. Honing our ability to help others and ourselves to not only weather the ups and downs of this limit and skill testing but also to *compassionately support* ourselves and others through those challenges is a must for athletes and coaches who want to get better.

Interestingly, when I have participants role-play how to support someone in emotional distress as part of my mental health awareness training programs, the most common error that helpers commit is to move too quickly from comfort and understanding into problem solving. This tendency appears to be a result of our discomfort in "merely" providing emotional support, as if that's not enough.

Yet, if we put ourselves in the place of the distressed person, we recognise the inevitable reality that, had the problem been easily solvable, we surely would have taken care of it already ourselves. And how does it feel when someone too quickly and without your permission tells you that they know exactly how you feel and have you tried XYZ solution? Most people, when I pose this question, readily agree that such interventions, even when delivered with good intent, can have a patronising, even disheartening effect—quite the opposite of what is usually intended.

People will also report that it's just weird or awkward to comfort someone they don't know well or at all. I often hear people say, "But I don't know what to say! What if I screw things up by saying the wrong thing?" I have been in rooms with athletes and coaches at a time when someone in the room was in distress. I watch as people look over at but do not acknowledge the person and avoid eye contact if possible. Then invariably, reproachful glances will be shot my way as if to say, "You're the psychologist—can't you just go and fix that? And make us all feel more comfortable?" The point here is that being compassionate is something anyone can do—and that it's likely to be more gratefully received from a trusted friend than by the on-site professional.

There is no one-size-fits-all recipe for compassion, although it would make my life teaching this concept easier if there were. What it does require is for us to relax and allow our prosocial instincts to care take over. Less can be more. It's about a comforting or supportive presence, and the willingness to lean into a conversation if the person is interested in talking about it. Silences are OK. The conversation is about the other person, not you or your story about the "even worse" situation you experienced (unless the other person asks for your advice). Instead, it can be useful to ask about what the other person has tried on their own to help themselves through their difficulty.

Standing with Yourself

When I suggest to people I work with that this resource, this support, is available to each of us in the form of *self-compassion*, I get reactions that range from shock to confusion to sheepishness. And invariably I hear words to the effect that *what we give so freely to others, we actively keep from ourselves or could never imagine doing*. Why? We don't think we deserve our own compassion, we can't even imagine doing it, never thought of it, or we think it will soften us up too much. We'll lose our drive (our grittiness!) or edge. We think this even though, logically, we can see that our words of kindness often have the opposite effect on others.

When people feel comforted, their suffering is eased—even slightly—because they know others care and understand. As a result, support like this, far from undermining effort, can actually help those who are suffering to find the energy or mojo to get back up and keep going. If this is true for others, surely it stands to reason that it would be true for ourselves.

Neuroscience supports this notion based on the discovery and increased understanding of an alternative system humans turn to in response to suffering. Most of us are aware of our "pleasure and reward" system mediated by the neurotransmitter dopamine—that feel-good response we get after eating sugar, taking risks and succeeding, or gambling and winning (to name a few examples). The problem with this system is that its positive effects are fleeting, putting us on a treadmill of needing more of these substances or activities to fuel the feel-good effects.

The alternative, called the "tend and befriend" system, is fed by oxytocin. Affectionately known as the "love" neurotransmitter, oxytocin is the hormone that makes hugs feel so good, and it is responsible for helping mothers and babies bond after birth. Not only that, but unlike the dopamine treadmill we can find ourselves on as we try to reproduce its fading effects, oxytocin produces more enduring positive effects on mood and well-being (Taylor, 2006). What triggers this system? Acts and thoughts of compassion—including self-compassion.

Let's assume that you are at least cautiously interested in this notion and willing to entertain a reality where self-compassion could play that counterintuitive, resilience-building role in your life. I'd argue that understanding that self-compassion is useful and important is not enough. Just like knowing what a balanced diet should be but not actually planning and eating healthy meals, theoretical understanding gets you only so far. This is exemplified by the people in workshops I teach who say to me, "Oh, I know I should be nicer to myself. So rather than beating up on myself after a mistake, I go right to problem-solving how the mistake happened so that I learn from it and move on."

Don't get me wrong: getting from character assassination to learning from mistakes is a big step, but it misses the step of self-compassion, of acknowledging the emotional suffering you are feeling having made the mistake in the first place. This was a game-changer for me, as I was one of those "be productive and keep going" folks myself. The first time I stopped to notice and actually experience the feelings—disappointment, embarrassment, to name a few—and then actually offer support to myself was an eye-opener. I just didn't know what I didn't know about the pain I was in and how it was hurting me.

Here's how Kristen Neff (2011), author of the aptly titled book *Self-Compassion*, describes this process as a way to enact self-compassion (see also Figure 6.2).

- **First, you want to notice your emotional experience, if any.** For me, it was often just a sense of heaviness I couldn't really explain.

- **Then you stop and (literally) put your hand on your heart and verbally acknowledge your feelings.** For me, the phrase "Whew, this is hard" was enough, because it *was* hard! The tone here is not of judgement, but of a simple, "right now, it's like this" acknowledgement.

- **Finally, say or think something supportive.** I resonate with "I'll be OK," but it could be whatever other supportive statement works for you. Others I have heard include "I've got this" and "I have my back." There's good evidence to suggest that even a small physical gesture of support, such as holding your hands together or placing a hand on your heart releases some of that feel-good oxytocin.

Note that I am not suggesting that you say, "It will *be* OK." I'm not a fan of saying things that I can't guarantee will be true. If the mistake was big enough, maybe it won't be OK—*but you can still be OK*. And in this small act of self-kindness and support, you can give to yourself some of what you may actually need the most.

----

* *After a mistake or failure, first become aware of your emotional experience in its aftermath, if any. Typical emotional reactions can include anger, disappointment, sadness, embarrassment, or anxiety.*

* *With that awareness, verbally acknowledge your feelings— "Whew, this is hard!" "That was tough!" or whatever phrase accurately acknowledges the feelings (without judgement). It is optional to hold your hands together or place your hand on your heart while you do this. Physical gestures such as these can enhance the experience and, as well, can trigger the release of beneficial hormones.*

* *Say or think something supportive. "I'll be OK," "I've got this," and "I have my back" are examples, but use the supportive statement that resonates with you.*

**Figure 6.2. Self-Compassion Practices:
What to Do after a Failure or Mistake**

The Inner Critic's Role as Sceptic and What You Can Do

I don't know a high-achieving athlete or coach who doesn't have an active inner critic—that voice in your head that kicks your tired butt out of bed and onto whatever training or other challenge awaits you. Having that "tell it straight and get to work" advisor working for you can be seen as one of the distinguishing characteristics of the highly gritty. Hooray!

This inner voice can be your best friend . . . until it is not. While its intentions are good—most inner dialogue is your mind's way of trying to keep you safe—sometimes your inner critique can take on a tone of criticism or even contempt that delivers the opposite of the intended effect. It's like the critic is still trying to help but has gone overboard into punishment. If this ever sounds like you, you are in good company; but I'd argue that critics that run amok in this way are not operating in our best interest, and it's up to us to regain the upper hand.

I mention this here because so often it is our inner critic that fights off the idea of self-compassion. Why should you be nice to yourself if you are lazy, a whiner, or a loser?

Paul Gilbert, professor of clinical psychology and the originator of compassion-focused therapy, poses some questions to ask yourself if you are interested in recalibrating your inner critic's approach and tone:

- **What does the critic actually feel about you?** That is, does it seem to you that your critic is on your side or against you? Does it like you?

- **What does the critic want to do to you?** Does it want you to succeed and is it helping you do so, or does it expect you to fail and is in fact counselling you in that direction?

- **Does the inner critic ever celebrate your successes?** If your inner critic was at all on your side, it would seem at least plausible that it would want to share your happiness as well as your disappointments. Sadly, I have never met an inner critic that balances its inputs in this way.

The point here is that, while most of us have inner critics, it's up to us as the thinking humans we are to decide if our critics are actually acting in our best interests or even want the best for us, or not.

And if you decide that your critic is not acting in your best interest, you have the power to start rebalancing that relationship. After all, your critic's stories are just thoughts. Not that any of this is easily undertaken, but a good first step is to simply do this work of more deeply unpacking your relationship with your inner critic, especially if its scepticism or contempt is holding you back from showing compassion to yourself.

Doing this work can be as simple (not necessarily easy) as gently rebuffing your critic. When you hear a criticism, you can even thank your critic for its opinion and then simply try on a more compassionate response. You hear: "You're such an idiot, you'll never get it right!" You say, "thanks for the thought. Yep, I made a mistake and that hurt, but it's not the end of the world. I'm still okay."

This is especially important as we contemplate the prospect of being kind to ourselves. The primary reason people turn away from self-compassion is a result of their inner critic's rejection of this idea as anything remotely worthwhile.

In closing, I challenge self-compassion sceptics to consider this act of making friends with yourself. The journey to excellence and optimal performance is long, often painful, and requires sacrifice, discipline, leaps of faith, facing our fears, and eyeballing the prospect of failure at every turn—and, dare I say, grit. Why would you want to make things even harder on yourself by being your own worst enemy, detractor, critic, or underminer? Another way to look at this? If you could not imagine treating your best friend this way, what makes it okay to do to yourself?

In the next section, we'll take our newfound self-compassion and flexible mindset further by exploring passion and its close cousin, purpose—the drivers that can allow us to stay even-keeled through even the most grit-inducing circumstances.

KEY TAKEAWAYS

✓ Going back to the *grit* basics (grit = passion + perseverance), if passion requires self-awareness and is something you think and feel, perseverance is all about behaviour.

✓ Making gritty performance *sustainable,* however, requires a third capability in addition to being aware of your passion and demonstrating perseverance in your behaviour, and that's self-compassion. Self-compassion fuels the resilience needed for sustained performance.

✓ If compassion is all about how we accept and support others when they are suffering, self-compassion is all that—turned inward.

✓ Many of us struggle to do compassion well, much less embrace the idea of being nice to ourselves.

✓ People resist self-compassion because they don't know how to do it, had not realized they needed it, did not think they deserved it, or think it will make them soft.

✓ Self-compassion practices can actually help us recover from failure or disappointment more quickly.

✓ Many high achievers have an inner critic, that inner voice that, when at its best, motivates us to get started and keep going.

✓ This inner critic can often, if we are not careful, tip over into punishing self-criticism and even contempt, which can erode confidence and self-regard.

✓ If your critic is unhelpful or worse, the goal is to rebalance your relationship with it and take back your power as an equal partner rather than subservient underling.

✓ Rebalancing means changing how you relate to your
   critic. Rather than simply accepting what it says, consider
   getting into a pleasant conversation, equal to equal. Gently
   challenging the evidence underpinning your critic's
   evaluations can also be useful.

PART III
INTRODUCTION TO PURPOSE

I n this section, we will explore another pillar underpinning the foundation of grit: the idea of *purpose*. In this context, I'm talking about a personal sense of purpose—a core ideal or philosophy that can guide our thinking, decisions, and behaviour. In so doing, I will be respectfully deviating away from Angela Duckworth's grit conceptualisation, augmenting (and when necessary, replacing) passion with purpose, and I will make the case for why this is justified.

Duckworth championed the combination of passion and perseverance as the two personal characteristics that differentiate people with grit from others. Given that her book was a result of her research exploring what seemed to underpin the efforts of people who strove and accomplished big, long-term goals, it is understandable how she landed there. Moreover, as her efforts to instil grit focus on children and helping them thrive, she (and they) are at a time in the lifespan when passions are more likely to be triggered and can be fostered.

My work with the already gritty, usually young adult to older athletes and coaches well into their life journeys, told me a slightly different tale. I found that, while passion is surely a gateway to grit, for a variety of reasons, it can lose its potency over the longer term. Its very volatility can make it less durable. For the already gritty, some adjustments might be needed.

With those realities in mind, here's what lies ahead.

- Chapter 7, "When Passion Is Not Enough," takes a closer look at the differences between passion and purpose, and why, in times of uncertainty or when we may be tempted to overindex on our grit, passion may actually not be fit for purpose. That is, while passion can be a powerful motivator, it can also be a capricious thing, and not everyone's adult "personal operating system" comes so equipped. Nor is passion necessarily static or long-lasting, even for those of us lucky enough to discover ours.

- Chapter 8, "Purpose as Antidote to Uncertainty," unpacks some of the facets underpinning purpose; explains why this concept is vital for us to explore for ourselves, particularly in times of change and uncertainty; and offers tools and strategies to get our purpose ball rolling.

- Finally, Chapter 9, "Enacting Purpose Through Service," looks at the landscape of service in times of uncertainty as well as how we can activate our purpose through serving—accurately and effectively—those we lead, work with, and care for.

7 WHEN PASSION IS NOT ENOUGH

In those times when our grit may not be enough, when our efforts feel harder or even pointless, it can be useful to look "under the hood" at what is fuelling our efforts and, as important, why. In this chapter, I explore how one of Angela Duckworth's grit foundations, passion, may not always even exist or serve us best as a driver toward more gritty effort.

Identifying and understanding our purpose—the *why* of our existence—may provide more useful motivational information. Purpose can effectively partner with passion but can also live on its own. You will learn about the pros and cons of passion, how purpose works and how it can even supplant passion, as well as ways you can hone your own sense of purpose.

The Lure of Passion

Why are well-meaning people always advising us to "follow our passion"? Because, in part, it's worth doing if you want to increase your odds of happiness and job satisfaction. It stands to reason that this would be so. If you find things you really like doing, your motivation for doing them and your willingness to stick with doing them even when things get difficult will be higher than for tasks you are not interested in.

Angela Duckworth is passionate about passion's role in understanding what motivates gritty people beyond the rest of us in their pursuit of Life's Important Goals. Here she is, describing what passion is during an interview with *Forbes* magazine's Dan Schawbel (2017):

> [Having] a **deep interest in your craft** is signature to grit. The people I study think about their work all the time because they're so incredibly **curious to learn more**. They **dream about what they do**. I do, too. Sometimes, when I get up in the middle of the night to get a drink of water, I find that I'm writing a paragraph in my head for a research article, or considering a new intervention idea, or replaying a snippet of conversation with a collaborator. I love what I do. **I don't love everything I have to do** to accomplish my top-level goal (use psychological science to help children thrive), but there is no other job in the world I would trade with my own. (emphasis added)

What I like about Duckworth's description is how she lets us know what we will experience when we are passionate. There is also a clear-eyed appreciation here for the fact that enacting your passion is not always easy and that you won't like some of the things you have to do to bring your passion to life.

But this is presuming that passion is "in the house" and that you have the wherewithal and the means to pursue it.

Giving Passion a Helping Hand

Duckworth, as a researcher who started out as an elementary school teacher, has advice she shared in her book on how children can (and should) start discovering and nurturing their passions. This makes sense if we walk backward from the notion of grit being that combination of passion and perseverance—that the first step for children, or anyone, really, who wants to achieve something good and hard, would be to find That Passionate Thing worth pursuing. Doing so would involve taking concrete steps to lean into those areas that interest us and cultivating those interests through closer examination and activity to see if one or more ignites into ambition that can't help but materialise into action.

Duckworth further suggests that parents should help, encourage, and even direct their children to "stick with" their interests for a quantifiable period of time—perhaps the entire duration of the class they enrolled them in to learn more about that thing—which has the simultaneous benefit of teaching them to practice gritty stick-to-it-ive-ness along the way.

This is all well and good—even great if, as a child, you had this kind of insight and support to help you identify and act on your deepest interests. I completely agree with and support Duckworth's contention that giving children permission and ample opportunities to explore and learn about what interests them should be a necessity, not a luxury, and that living a life where we have the opportunity to, as the saying goes, follow our passion, is truly a life more likely to be well-lived.

What If Passion Just Doesn't Exist?

For many adults I know, however, passion is not, nor has it ever been, a reality, much less something to follow. There are a multitude of reasons, both personal and environmental. For some of us, and I count myself among them, it can be about having too many interests. For others, the gap between one's interests and gainful employment can feel like "a bridge too far" and unworkable, while still others never really allowed themselves—or were allowed—to contemplate their true interests.

I also wonder if "passion following" has a cultural bias as well. I have noticed in Australia, for example, as compared to the United States, where I am from, there is a more pragmatic, straightforward, and dare I say directive approach to higher education. As my child was finishing up her high school years, the big questions weren't, "What are you interested in?" or "What are you thinking of studying?" but "What are you going to *be*?" It felt to me like there was less tolerance for 17-year-olds still being unsure of their career direction. And I am curious to know if this desire for certitude may be foreclosing, for some students, that exploration and search for one's passion.

Other Roadblocks to Passion

In my work, both in and out of sport, however, I regularly come across people who, even if they know what it is, have yet to act on their passion. The most common reason for this? Fear. Fear of failure, fear of success (!), fear of disappointing others who have a different idea about what our lives should look like. With fear comes anxiety and worry, both of which are often alleviated by delaying or denying that which worries us. If we are afraid to try out for a sport or apply to graduate school and thus procrastinate and miss or avoid the try-out and application, the fear goes away and we feel better immediately. As well, the passion remains available to play with in our mind's eye—but inactivated: "I *could* be great but choose not to."

Sometimes our passion inaction is due to a lack of awareness, belief, or the resources to make a go of it. In some cases, however, we are living a shadow life—one in which we may be aware of our passion but may be playing only peripherally around its edges. It's as if we are afraid to pursue our passion but mask that by doing something "kind of like" the thing we are passionate about.

Consider, for example, the fictional but still appropriate example of Nathan in the TV show *Ted Lasso*: Nathan dreams of putting his days as an equipment manager behind him and stepping into the role of a soccer coach, but instead of acting on those ideas, he contents himself with talking about what he would do if he were the coach. That is, until Ted Lasso comes along. But let's not spoil the story.

Steven Pressfield (2012), author of the book *Turning Pro*, calls this "shadow ambition"—that place of inadvertent complacency where it can look like we are doing what we love, but instead we have crafted an imitation version of our life's passion. If selling other people's music is your vibe, then fine, but if you reckon you were put on this Earth to create music and have contented yourself with just selling the creations of others, then perhaps it's time to give your passion a whirl.

The passion "risk" for anyone in a field where talent is king (such as elite sport) is when we are so rewarded for our talents that we forget or minimize our other passions, or we are actively discouraged from pursuing them. The extreme here is the talented athlete who is not passionate about her sport but succeeds anyway, due to her talent, despite just going through the motions.

For others, economic circumstances or a lack of opportunity may have rendered the idea of "doing what you are interested in" completely moot. If my family is living hand to mouth, it can feel downright pretentious and self-absorbed to hold out for my passion to ignite or spend time trying to find out what it is.

The Interweaving of Passion and Purpose

As an avid athlete and college senior interested in psychology, my passion was ignited when I discovered that there was a field actually called *sport* psychology. Once I found out that there was a way to knit together my interest in psychology with my love for sport, I was off to the races. My then-insatiable curiosity and interest fuelled me through a master's degree, a doctorate degree, and into a career working for the US Olympic Committee (USOC) and then for the Australian Institute of Sport (AIS).

Interestingly, I didn't feel the need for a purpose through these years and never even thought to question it—this despite burning out of my USOC role, spending six months recovering (not enough time, it turned out), but then eventually having it rekindle through my leadership role with the AIS. Without realising it, I was resuscitating my passion by changing my purpose.

It was only after leaving the AIS, though, that I gave serious thought to not just "what now?" but "why?" "Why do I do what I do, and what does that mean going forward?" The purpose game-changer for me was in adding the values of sustainability and happiness to the high-performance equation. These were largely missing in my own professional life, I realised. I suffered burnout, exhaustion, and periods of significant personal self-doubt at the altar of drive. Talk about grit gone wrong! It was in the recognition of what was missing and using it to define my personal and professional purpose that things shifted most profoundly. And that clarity of purpose—using my expertise in performance psychology to help others attain more sustainable high performance *and* happier lives—has sustained me (and my passion) ever since.

Is Passion Overrated?

So it's an interesting and sometimes complex relationship between passion and purpose. Which begs the question, do you need both or either? Harvard Business School professor Jon Jachimowicz (2019) studies the role of passion in work success. His research in this space should provide comfort to those who haven't experienced the siren song of passion and think they are either deficient or somehow doomed to less satisfaction (and if they believe in grit, less of that) in pursuit of life's big goals.

He offers these insights into why it may be actually *inappropriate* to follow your passion:

- Passion is not something you find, but rather, it is something to be developed.
- It is challenging to pursue your passion, especially as it wanes over time.
- Passion can also lead you astray, and it is therefore important to recognize its limits.

Developing (as opposed to discovering) your passion means spending more time exploring the tasks that pique your curiosity and working more closely with those who inspire you. It also helps to get to know your colleagues, what they are passionate about, and how they view what they do through that lens.

Jachimowicz suggests further that, rather than seeing your passion as something you *love*, you consider focusing on what you *care about*. This subtle distinction is meaningful: focusing on what you love associates passion with what you enjoy and what makes you happy, whereas focusing on what you care about aligns passion with your values and the impact you want to have. This shift, as a matter of fact, is where we are headed in the next chapter as we consider the transition from passion to purpose.

Scott Brennan, the gritty rower we met in Chapter 2,

had this to say about the relationship among grit, passion, and purpose:

> *Let's talk about grit. You can have the same person and you can change their level of grit easily. So, you can say to me, "Go run 100 kilometres now, in these clothes." I'm going to say, "No way." You say, "OK, go run 100 kilometres now and I will give you a million dollars to do it." Or hold a gun to my head: "Go run 100 kilometres now." Or, hold it to my son's head. Like, I'll run 200 kilometres. And I will still come back and kill you afterwards. . . .*

> *It's that idea of a driving force. What is it that you're after? And that's not necessarily passion to a degree. It's because passion is, by its very definition, this tempestuous, volatile thing. But when people were kind of searching for this grit, it's the grind down, down, down. So it's not passion, because passion flares up and it's gone. It's great for "heat of the moment" stuff, you know. But most of the grit stuff is like, "How are you going to grind this out for one year, two years? The rest of your life, whatever—I don't know." That's where it kind of comes more into that purpose.*

Purpose Can Be (and Often Is) Enough

So if passion is not all that it's cracked up to be, or if we simply don't feel passionate about that One Grand Idea, are we destined for a life less well-lived? Fear not. Research in the area of sustained work success suggests that identifying and intentionally living your purpose provides a more sustainable fuel source than passion alone (Pearce, 2019).

Purpose in this context includes the following:

- **What?** (What am I interested in/curious about?)
- **Why?** (Why is this important for or needed in the world?)
- **Why me?** (How will I serve the world in this space?)
- **How?** (What values drive my service?)

Note that, defined in this way, our purpose gives our passion direction and beyond that, is outward-focused in the sense that it seeks to *serve*. How do I want to channel myself in service to others, to the world? What problems am I most interested in solving? What suffering do I want to relieve? Leaders and coaches who define their *why* in this way find it easier to inspire others to follow. People who do this kind of purpose exploration and live by a coherent life purpose literally live longer (Hill & Turiano, 2014).

Applying these standards to my own life, I serve the world by helping people show up, perform, and relate with less friction, more sustainability, and more happiness, qualities I firmly believe the world needs more of. My background in elite sport, particularly in seeing the negative consequences for athletes and coaches when sustainability and happiness were not valued or accounted for, gives me the courage of my convictions. I advocate, educate, coach, and counsel with kindness and compassion for the people I work with and care about.

I hope this chapter has persuaded you that even if, for whatever reason, a passion has eluded you, you can still intentionally craft a purpose worth pursuing. And if you *are* passionate about your life's work, honing your passion through a prism of purpose—asking yourself the *what, why, why me,* and *how* questions—can give additional clarity to your efforts.

The next chapter illustrates the signature role that purpose plays in times of change and uncertainty. As well, we unpack the nuts and bolts you need to craft your own purpose that is more "fit for purpose."

KEY TAKEAWAYS

✓ Passion is a great accelerator in the grit equation, but what happens if you don't have one? While we can help children find passion, for many adults, there are legitimate reasons why passion not only doesn't exist, but the opportunity to discover one is unrealistic or unavailable.

✓ Reasons people don't have or pursue their passion include a lack of (1) awareness as to what their passion is, (2) belief that the passion is worth pursing, and (3) the resources to follow their passion. The most common block is fear.

✓ As popularly conceived, finding one's passion is an inexact science at best and can wax and wane over time.

✓ A useful adjunct or even substitute for passion is purpose:

the answer to the questions such as, Why I am here? Why do I do what I do? Purpose can drive behaviour even in the absence of passion.

✓ Focusing on what you love associates passion with what you enjoy and what makes you happy, whereas focusing on what you care about aligns passion with your values and the impact you want to have—transforming it into purpose.

✓ Research looking at sustained work success suggests that identifying and intentionally living your purpose provides a more sustainable source of motivation than passion alone.

✓ Purpose in this context includes the following:
   ◦ **What?** (What am I interested in/curious about?)
   ◦ **Why?** (Why is this important for or needed in the world?)
   ◦ **Why me?** (How will *I* serve the world in this space?)
   ◦ **How?** (What values drive my service?)

8 PURPOSE AS ANTIDOTE TO UNCERTAINTY

In the last chapter, you learned about the limitations of passion and how having a sense of purpose can augment or even serve in the absence of passion. Here, I flesh out the idea of "purpose" more fully and explain why it can be a literal antidote to the vicissitudes of uncertainty. Moreover, you'll receive specific strategies and practices that will help you start to craft your own sense of purpose.

What Is Purpose, Exactly?

The *Oxford English Dictionary* offers these definitions for the word *purpose*:

> **Noun:** the reason for which something is done or created or for which something exists; a person's sense of resolve or determination.
> **Verb:** have as one's intention or objective.

Both forms, noun and verb, resonate. Together, they convey the value of purpose, particularly when we are faced with uncertainty and change. Our environment can shift and change, but what we stand for does not. How we choose to think or behave does not. This sense of a core stability offers a counterbalance to the unease, anxiety, or hypervigilance that uncertainty invariably stirs up for us human beings. Psychologist after psychologist I interviewed extolled the mental health benefits, the increased resilience, and the motivational boost that purpose can provide.

We heard Scott Brennan in Chapter 7 distinguish purpose from passion in a way that makes intuitive sense to the coaches and athletes I speak with. That is, passion has a capricious quality to it, with the attendant risk being that it can come and go. Losing interest and passion can be—and is often—a reason why athletes retire from their sport.

Purpose, on the other hand, can partner with and direct passion's energy but can also live on its own. Purpose, in this context, is driven as much if not more by our values—those qualities we hold most dear and want to live in accordance with—as it is by our interests or passions.

Values, as opposed to passions, are those stable, aspirational qualities that we strive for, that make us feel good when we embody them, or that make us uncomfortable when we realize we do not. Values have a sense of durability that passion may not have. We do not tick a value box, never to revisit it again. It sounds ridiculous to even think that, if we value honesty as a quality to strive for, we'd ever reach a point of saying, "Enough honesty already!"

As a sport psychologist, I have sometimes operated as a "values checker" for coaches and athletes, helping them to see where they are living in accordance with what they value—and, as important, where there's a disconnect. Examples include the coaches who pride themselves on being good communicators but have not made time for their athletes, or the athlete who points to her work ethic but has started cutting corners in training.

Why Is Purpose So Important?

The durability of purpose is one of its superpowers. In my interviews with performance psychologists on this topic, they tended to use one of two metaphors to illustrate how purpose worked: as either a "North Star" or a boat anchor. Purpose sat like a guiding star above what we were doing and became a way to keep our journey on point; or, if we were a boat in a storm, our purpose acted to keep our prow pointing into the wind and preventing a capsize, no matter the weather. Whatever the imagery employed, their message was this: having a purpose adds a sense of stability and inner direction when the environment is too uncertain or chaotic to provide them.

Without the rudder of purpose in tough times, here are some mistakes I've seen athletes and coaches make. One problem is when we confuse speed with accuracy in decision making—that is, defaulting to making impulsive, even ill-considered decisions just to appear decisive and presumably lessening the perceived angst of indecision—for ourselves or those we lead.

Or, coaches and athletes myopically revert to their strengths—the things that always used to work—without considering if what they always have done is actually the most appropriate action for right now. The mistake? Mistaking action for purpose.

Conversely, in times of change, we can waffle with indecision. This tendency was more prevalent during the early days of Covid lockdowns, when athletes were isolated from their coaches and normal training routines. At first, throwing off the yoke of a daily routine can feel downright refreshing—"Finally, I can do what I want, when I want!"—but sometimes it leads to decision fatigue. Without structure or a plan, each day presents a new chance to procrastinate and second-guess: "Should I train now? Later? What do l feel like? Is this the best time? What about later?"

The value of purpose in these situations is in its ability to provide a bigger picture, the ability to step back and consider what's needed from me and for others right now. This is not to say that qualities like "hard work" aren't useful; but without a purpose standing behind it that answers the *why* question, without intention and direction, mindless "hard work" may well take us in the wrong direction.

A second purpose superpower? Its very intentionality. While passion either hits us or is otherwise unearthed by us, we get to *craft* our purpose. Through the exploration process I will outline later in this chapter, we can work on our purpose. And with this intentional building comes the ability to tweak and change as circumstances dictate.

A Story of Life Purpose Found and Passion Harnessed

Mental performance coach, author, and facilitator Cindra Kamphoff told me the story about the event that compelled her to come out from her shadow existence, to activate her passion with purpose. At the time, Cindra was a professor and researcher in sport psychology as well as an avid marathoner. She had just finished the 2013 Boston Marathon when all hell broke loose—loud noises followed by masses of panicked people running *away* from the finish line ahead of billowing smoke—a result of bombs detonated by domestic terrorists. Fearing for her life, Cindra made her way back to her hotel. With no cell phone coverage, news was slow to come by, and she wondered if she was safe and if she would ever see her children again.

> I mean, talk about fear! I didn't know if I was going to get home to see my two boys, and to be honest, you know, my running didn't matter. What mattered most was my family, and what mattered second was my purpose. Once we found out there was not a bomb in our hotel, that we were safe in our hotel room, I just remember sitting in that hotel room and asking myself these questions. It was like, "Why am I here?" and "What difference do I make?" and "Why do I do what I do?" That day, I'm grateful for. You might think like, "Why? You're grateful for being at the Boston Marathon bombing?" But it woke me up to my purpose, and it woke me up to why I'm here.

Since 2013, I've been making very different changes in my life. I was teaching and doing research, and now I'm doing more consulting; I have my own business; I wanted to write a book; and I wanted to work with a pro team. And so my life is drastically changed, mostly because I was able to instil and really connect with my purpose every day.

Taking Your Purpose from Intention to Behaviour

Life events bigger than we are—in Cindra's case, the Boston Marathon bombing, or say, 9/11—can often serve as catalysts for life change and a reorientation of purpose. As Cindra suggested, just the thought of being unsafe was enough to compel her to question what was important—not "finishing a marathon," for sure—and home in on "Why am I here?"

Not everyone experiences a cataclysmic personal or life event that so starkly puts everything that is important to them into perspective. My intent, in fact, is to save you the time and the anguish by suggesting that this kind of inquiry can and should periodically be done no matter your situation—personal, pandemic-related, or otherwise. So wherever you are, whatever your situation, here are the steps.

The question "Why do I do what I do?" informs us about what we like about, value, or are dissatisfied with in our current situation, including the idea that maybe we do what we do because we are afraid—of change, of failure, of even success.

Mining for Your Life Purpose

Here are some strategies, based in part on suggestions from Richard Leider (2015), author of *The Power of Purpose*, to help you clarify your life purpose:

1. Write down your "Big Event" lifeline: What were the important or "standout" events in your life? Alternatively, reflect back on your life in five-year increments. What was happening when you were 5, 10, 15 years old, and beyond? Write down what happened, what it meant to you at the time, and the significance it holds now.

2. What are your gifts and talents? If you don't know, ask friends and family to tell you.

3. What activities and pursuits do you *love* doing?

4. What's *worth* caring about or doing? What issues, interests, causes, or curiosities capture your enthusiasm?

5. What are your core values—those aspirational qualities that light you up and make you want to be a better person? Tip: pick out no more than five; otherwise, nothing is prioritized. (To get you started, the Appendix contains a list of values developed by James Clear, author of *Atomic Habits*.)

Once you complete these reflections, what emerges? Do you detect themes? Underlying motivations? What insights emerge from your successes and, even more important, your failures? Then try your hand at writing a few purpose statements. It is so often true that it is in your third and fourth efforts that your truth starts to emerge. For example, if you've identified "kindness" as a core value, your purpose statement might be "I will strive to treat people, both those I know and strangers, kindly every day through my words and actions."

What Cindra Kamphoff's story also brings to life is the idea that it is *not* enough to be able to answer those questions clearly, to identify that craft that you are really, truly, deeply interested in. It is not enough to be curious or continually immersed. Cindra describes an intentionality to her purpose, that it is not enough to know what it is, but to connect and reconnect with that purpose every day.

Doing this exploration takes work and time, which is a deterrent for even those of us who want to discern our life's meaning (much less those of us who have yet to realize that this might be a good idea). Yet, I ask, what's the alternative? How does denying ourselves the gift of purpose serve the world? George Bernard Shaw puts it this way:

> This is the true joy in life, being used for a purpose recognized by yourself as a mighty one. Being a force of nature instead of a feverish, selfish little clod of ailments and grievances, complaining that the world will not devote itself to making you happy. I am of the

opinion that my life belongs to the whole community
and as long as I live, it is my privilege to do for it what
I can. I want to be thoroughly used up when I die, for
the harder I work, the more I live. I rejoice in life for its
own sake. Life is no brief candle to me. It is a sort of
splendid torch which I have got hold of for the moment
and I want to make it burn as brightly as possible
before handing it on to future generations. (Shaw, 2008)

Being and staying gritty is hard enough. You don't want to find out you were headed in the wrong direction or working hard for the wrong reason. Getting your purpose right increases your grit "efficiency" by clarifying where you're heading, every day.

When Uncertainty Strikes: Pivoting Purpose

In times of uncertainty, we want to learn how to read our environment accurately and consider how we can move through it effectively. And that might mean revisiting what we are about amidst the changing realities we are facing, and perhaps even shifting our purpose. It's not an either/or proposition, for relying on our core values can steady us and keep us stable. But rather, it's about keeping that rudder in the water while answering these questions: What's my purpose *in this time?* Why am I here, doing this, now?

Here are the steps to help you determine your "fit for purpose" purpose:

1. Accurately assess what's happening around you.

On a factual level, what are the challenges and the realities you're facing? Taking the Covid pandemic as an example, sports were facing a myriad of challenges: how to keep people healthy and safe, complying with state and federal direction about lockdown restrictions, loss of revenue and competitions, and how to support athletes appropriately and realistically as they were no longer engaged in centralised training. Coaches were concerned for their own futures as well as for their athletes. Sport staff were scrambling to find and get resources out to anyone who they thought might benefit.

The first step in attaining "reality accuracy" is recognising the various impacts the situation may be having. Make a list of everything you can think of—financial, resource-related, physical, mental, infrastructural, time impacts—knowing that no list will be complete. Who could have predicted, for example, the global supply chain crisis at the beginning of the pandemic?

Then, to the extent you're able, consider the varying impact of those events you just listed on the different people and groups you are interacting with. Not everyone will be impacted the same way, for example, by the notion of potential stand-downs in an organisation. People in the same group may well be differently impacted by the same set of changes or stressors. During the pandemic, some athletes thrived on their own, away from the one-size-fits-all training regime, able or skilled enough to give themselves what they needed to train well, if not better than when they were back with their teammates. Others, on the other hand, struggled with the constant decisions to be made in the absence of structure and suffered without teammates to benchmark against.

The third and most important work to do in this space is to talk with all those impacted, without bias or prejudice, about how they are faring. What are the opportunities and threats they see or are facing?

The importance of this third step cannot be overstated. We can all too often fall into the trap of assuming we know how a person is doing because of our shared history (under perhaps more reliable circumstances and over long periods of time) or basing our assessment on old data. Many athletes and coaches I spoke to about the effects of the pandemic were in fact surprised by their own unexpected responses. If they themselves are surprised, it's highly likely that we won't have much luck predicting how they will cope or how they are feeling. Ask them.

This assessment of your current reality (summarized in Figure 8.1) is not just about what is actually happening. It is also about how it is impacting the people you care about, work with, and, in the case of coaches, the athletes you're responsible for training. While both aspects are important, from a psychological standpoint, as a sport psychologist, I am focused primarily on the latter—the impact of any uncertainty or change on each person as well as the group as a whole. Here are some impact identification and assessment steps that can help you get started:

1. Brainstorm impacts of the situation: financial, resource-related, physical, mental, infrastructural, time-related, geographic.

2. Estimate the power of each impacting factor on individuals and groups.

3. Check in with each individual to find out how they are doing and explore other potential impacts not considered.

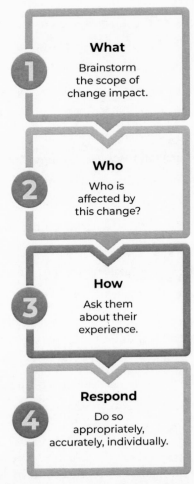

Figure 8.1. Steps to Assess and Respond to Change

2. *Respond appropriately, accurately, and individually.*

Now that we've evaluated the impact on ourselves and people around us, we take action in the spirit of service to meet people where they are, not where we are used to them being or where we would like them to be. It's not just about the fact that, under conditions of change and uncertainty, people react differently, but that they do so in uniquely individual ways.

A Story About Assessing and Responding to Change

When Covid first made its presence known in mid-2020, I interviewed several coaches to find out how they were coping during the pandemic, including University of Arizona and two-time Olympic women's softball coach Mike Candrea. His story inspired my thinking in this space.

During our interview, I was expressing curiosity about his team's use of sport psychology to enhance performance in light of a likely reduced competition schedule, when Coach Candrea put up his hand to stop me.

> *It's not about performance right now. I'm most concerned about everyone's welfare and mental health.*

He told me about how he and his staff would check in regularly on athletes from a health and well-being perspective. They instituted periodic townhall-style meetings to answer questions from naturally concerned parents and created a community of support around the athletes.

Candrea went on to describe a situation of unintended consequences created when the National Collegiate Athletic Association (NCAA, the U.S. governing body for university sport) gifted an extra year of college eligibility to allow fourth-year athletes the opportunity to play an extra season after the 2020 season was cancelled. While this was an act of generosity for that final-year cohort, it disadvantaged the underclass athletes who'd been anticipating cracking the starting line-up for their final year. Coaches could be excused for seeing this as a boon—the chance to hoard all this extra talent. Instead, Candrea and his staff checked in with all their underclass players to gauge their interest in remaining on the roster, assisted any player who wanted to find a better-fit university team situation, and facilitated the transfer process.

Staff also went out of their way to see that fun and enjoyment were a priority. Practices were restructured to focus on team-building games as much as skill building. Impromptu trips out for ice cream became part of the routine.

You'd be forgiven for wondering why Coach Candrea and his staff would go to this amount of trouble in ways that had nothing to do with performance. But really, what was the alternative? The pandemic forced shutdowns and slowdowns. Rather than fighting them or pretending they didn't exist, this program saw opportunities to care for athletes in a variety of ways, strengthening relationships with individuals and families while prioritizing well-being in a time of massive uncertainty.

If fairy tales really came true, the next thing you'd hear is that the University of Arizona went on in their next season to win it all in the 2021 Women's College World Series. Instead, the 11th-ranked Arizona Wildcats were ousted in two hard-fought games, losing their final game against Florida State by a run in the bottom of the last inning. Nevertheless, here is what senior player Maliah Martinez had to say about her coach after the game:

> I feel like I'm forever indebted to coach [Candrea]. He really has had such an impact on my life and has really built me into the person I am both on and off the field. He's always there for me, and I just love that man so much and owe him everything. I'm just grateful for the opportunity to be able to play for him.

This chapter has shown how to seek out, build, and pivot your purpose when circumstances demand it. In the next chapter, I take the idea of purpose and talk about how to activate it for ourselves, by tapping into our human need to be in service, as well as ways to be of best-fit service to those we lead, work with, and love.

KEY TAKEAWAYS

✓ Purpose is defined as one's "reason for being;" one's intentions or objective.

✓ The idea of purpose is particularly useful in times of uncertainty or change, as it conveys a sense of internal stability, like a personal North Star or the anchor that keeps one's prow heading into the wind.

✓ While passion is more closely associated with a strong emotional connection to something, purpose is more closely aligned with one's values.

✓ Common mistakes we make when times are tough, when we lack purpose, are confusing fast decisions with good decisions, rigidly sticking to a preferred way of acting in the world without due consideration for what's actually happening, or conversely, waffling with indecision.

✓ Uncovering your purpose can be as simple as periodically asking the questions "Why am I here?" and "Why do I do what I do?" then thoughtfully listening to what comes up for you. A more detailed step-by-step process is included at the end of this chapter.

✓ No purpose is immune from the need to change. Rather, it can be important to pivot one's purpose to meet the situation's changing needs.

✓ In times of change, here are the steps to take to help keep your purpose relevant to the evolving reality:
  ○ Accurately assess the situation at hand. Brainstorm the scope of the impact, *identify who is affected by the change, and talk to them directly about how they are doing and find out what they need.*
  ○ Respond appropriately, accurately, and individually.

✓ Consider this process to clarify your life's purpose:
  ○ Write down your "big event life timeline."
  ○ Identify your gifts and talents.
  ○ What are the activities and pursuits you love doing?
  ○ What's worth caring about or doing?
  ○ What are your core values?

9 ENACTING PURPOSE THOUGH SERVICE

In 2020, as Covid reared its head across the world, my own practice, along with so many other businesses, took a nose-dive. Early lockdowns made in-person workshops and consultations—the bread and butter of my business—untenable. At the same time, I was consumed with the idea of wanting to make a positive difference for so many others who were suffering through the profound fear and uncertainty brought on by those early "shock and awe" days of Covid. I conceived the idea to interview performance psychologists about how they helped people learn to thrive in uncertainty and then share these learnings with the public.

When I tested this idea with my psychologist colleagues, I found that I was not alone in my thinking. Everyone was more than happy to help, support, or serve as an interviewee. In the end, 20 psychologists from around the world agreed to be interviewed. Having no idea what I was doing, I spent my first two government-assistance relief payments to hire an event-management company to help me pull off the event.

Dreaming up the idea, taking the risk, investing significant time and money, and hosting this event totally rocked my world. Never before had I experienced the execution of a purpose I could get completely behind so clearly and emphatically. This impact was unanticipated, but it taught me a powerful personal lesson about how crafting and executing something I believed in so strongly could become the being-in-service antidote I didn't know I needed at the time.

When in times of uncertainty (and all the time, frankly) we can move out of our own sense of fear and threat, or our own myopic self-focus, and lean into understanding the suffering of others in order to find a way to serve them where they are, we most certainly serve ourselves. Coaches, staff, and organisations that find ways to thrive through uncertainty almost invariably do so when their efforts are focused through the prism of service. "If in doubt, how can I best serve those around me?"

And while this idea of being in service to others may not, at first blush, feel relevant for athletes, I'd argue otherwise. Stepping outside one's individual pursuit of excellence to be in service to one's peers, training partners, and even opponents brings perspective and humility into the picture, if we let it.

To serve well requires an understanding of what service is required. To start this process in the context of helping others thrive in uncertainty, let's unpack how people typically react to those conditions. By understanding their needs, we increase our chances of effective service. At the same time, this exercise is also for *you*. As you read through the reactions described in the next section, can you see yourself in any of them? Having that base sense of empathy and understanding will serve you well as you serve others.

Reactions to Uncertainty

Figure 9.1 represents the most common ways people respond to uncertainty, as culled from my experience as well from as my interviews with performance psychologists.

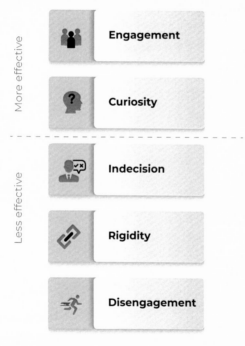

Figure 9.1. Common Human Reactions to Threat and Uncertainty

The order of reactions, from bottom to top, reflects their relative degree of coping effectiveness. If we think back to how our brains were evolutionarily wired to respond to threat, this starts to make sense. Viewing these responses through our "4 F" threat responses discussed in Chapter 3, disengagement could be seen as a form of fleeing, rigidity as a form of fighting, and indecision as a form of freezing. Curiosity and engagement, on the other hand, represent more functional and flexible responses. Let's unpack them further.

Disengagement

Disengaged individuals have essentially "checked out." This reaction could be likened to a form of learned helplessness in which they think not only that they do not have control, but also that the situation and the way it is being handled are diverging ever further from their own personal sense of purpose. They stop investing emotionally and are preparing themselves for at least the possibility of leaving the situation entirely. This could be seen as a form of self-protection. "I'm no longer investing emotionally, see no hope (or even if there is some, it's too little, too late), and am preparing for the worst and planning for and starting to invest in a future without this."

Rigidity

In this case, people may be literally denying reality, in the sense that they are reactive and angry about a situation completely out of their control. "I'm so pissed at the shutdowns, the changes, that my 2020 Olympic dream was taken from me. After I made the team, too!" That may all be true, but it's simply not a very useful or productive state of mind. This kind of emotionality perpetuates one's pain and suffering, by keeping it alive. There is no point in trying to argue the point. People in this space are prone to grudgingly accepting reality for a time but then being pulled back into the injustice of it all. The fire that burns here burns best when there is a group of like-minded people with whom to fan the flames of outrage. This kind of reactive anger can also function like a shield against less acceptable fear. If I stay angry, I don't feel sad, worried, afraid, or heartbroken.

Indecision

For some people, lack of structure coupled with a lack of experience, discipline, or confidence can lead to indecision. Some athletes who initially gravitated to the idea of no coach to watch over them and no training regime to follow found themselves at a loss when it came to self-organising each day, every day. This led to disrupted sleep cycles that bled into the following day, changing wake times with flow-on effects throughout the day, only to worsen by night-time. Indecision played out for coaches, too, who were thrust out of their comfort zones trying to write programs for an entirely novel fifth quadrennium for athletes whose ongoing fitness was unknown, and for competition cycles that came and went as pandemic hotspots flared and receded. "What do I do—is this right? Good enough?" "Should I train now? . . . What about now?" "How?"

Curiosity

Getting curious about a novel situation, particularly one that is seen as having the potential to upend our livelihood or threaten our health and that of our loved ones, is not a typical first port of call for most athletes and coaches. But it can be a healthy shift away from our very human tendency to see uncertainty as the enemy or something to be feared. Living in those states of mind is corrosive to our well-being after a time, as well as being unsustainable over the long haul, and can lead to the sense of disengagement that topped this list.

Ah, but curiosity? Getting to this point in the way one sees uncertainty may well be a tipping point, where an athlete who has been worried about maintaining her fitness outside of a group structure realises that she has found a way to regularly train that works even better. And maybe for the first time she starts to trust her judgment and knowledge about what she actually needs rather than what she has been told to do.

Once this point has been reached, what used to be threatening and lacking (in normalcy, stability, predictability) becomes an opportunity to explore. "Interesting! When I back off a little and improve my flexibility, my reach and flow really increase! I wonder . . ." Coaches and staff, with curiosity, can look at training and support with fresh eyes—out of the box labelled "How It Always Has Been Done, " away from knee-jerk reaction to threat, and into a more open-eyed appraisal of potential opportunity.

A final word about curiosity. There are various forms of it, not all equally useful. I broached this idea in Chapter 5, but it's worth a revisit here. Riffing from Jud Brewer's (2021) excellent treatise on this distinction in his book *Unwinding Anxiety*, I distinguish between "kind" curiosity and "why" curiosity. In kind curiosity, we are merely taking an interest in something, as in "How interesting that every time I wonder what will happen in my upcoming performance, my self-talk turns negative and undermining." This quality of curiosity can be a game-changer for those of us used to judging the heck out of ourselves, when we can make that shift from judgment to exploration.

On the flip side is "why" curiosity. This is the curiosity that asks the why questions, as in "Why do I keep doing this to myself?" or "Why am I such an idiot?" This type of curiosity is our judging mind's exceptionally crafty U-turn right back to self-judgment, which is its forte, after all. It's as if, in discovering this truth about ourselves, something essential and life-changing will be revealed: "Once I understand *why* things are like they are, all will be well." The reality is, satisfying this curiosity rarely leads anywhere useful. So when I talk about curiosity in this context, it's about that kind curiosity that asks opportunity-opening questions, not the corrosive "Why are these things happening to me?" curiosity.

Engagement

Engagement is curiosity with momentum. Curiosity is not inherently wise. Not all of our thoughts and plans that deviate from the norm into the possibilities offered up by uncertainty are functional or worthwhile. We increase our chances of success through the accurate reading of our environments and of the people within them and *then* trying something different. The more we know about what's going on around us, the more accurate our innovation can be. Hitting that curiosity sweet spot where we discover something new which works *and* builds and sustains our momentum. We have found a new way to work . . . that works. This type of engagement can be at the individual as well as the organizational level.

Bronwen Knox, four-time Olympian in water polo, talks here about her own curiosity and "out-of-the-box thinking" early in her career that challenged the systems and her coaches' way of slotting players into narrow "speciality" roles:

> Way back early in my career, back in 2007 when I was going for my first Olympics, it was "This is your position, this is your role on the team, this is what you're here to do." Nothing else. And I found that really closed-minded and very specific. And I sat down with the coaches and said, "Well, what if this doesn't work? What if I need to adapt and evolve and be more than one thing?" And they're like, "No, we just need you for this thing." And I walked away and thought about it more. I said, "Well, if I want to make this team, I'm going to have to be really good at that. And if I want to be one of the best players, I'm going to have to be really good at a lot of things, and it's going to be a slow journey, and it's going to be time and time again going back to the drawing board and checking in." And I think over time I'm now in a position like with these Olympic Games, my fourth Olympic Games, I played three or four different positions, which was hard in itself because you sort of never know really where you sat.
>
> But it's something that made me probably more valuable to this team. I could actually sit almost anywhere in the pool in the team and contribute to the highest level possible. So I think that, to me, was one of the things I was really glad I stepped out of that box early on in my career, because if I had to stay in there, I

don't know if I'd be here today and be in the position I am today,
because, purely on team selection, team dynamics, you don't
want to have too many of one and not enough of the other. But
being someone who's mobile and can move around any position is
a commodity that we just don't see.

This story illustrates the power of curiosity as well as the tenacity it can take not only to expand one's skill sets in these ways, but to wear down a system not used to this idea to get that mutual sense of engagement.

Serving Others Accurately and Effectively

Serving others is one thing. Doing so in a way that meets them where they are and accurately meets their needs is another. Let's consider how we can serve based on the reaction-to-uncertainty states shown in Figure 9.1. It stands to reason that we don't interact with a despondent athlete about to disengage in the same way we might with the rigid athlete angrily railing against reality. Yet, how often do we see a group of distressed people treated in a one-size-fits-all manner?

Preparing your service mindset and creating safe space

The universal first step is to invite dialogue and be prepared to listen carefully and completely. The goal here is accurate understanding of what the person in front of you is going through. For a coach meeting up with a disgruntled or despondent athlete, it can be an ego-threatening business.

Athletes will disengage because they have lost hope, which means in some way, shape, or form, there has been an existing disconnection that is now threatening relationship rupture and disengagement. Confronting, withstanding, and moving to a conversation where the disengaged and perhaps bitter person feels heard can feel daunting. But learning these skills can make coaches and staff better leaders, parents, colleagues . . . and people.

A couple tips here. The first is to signal your intent early on that you want to fully understand the situation from the other person's point of view. And stick to that. The job here is to make the conversation a safe one and to keep it that way. Allowing someone to explore their discontent in this safe way can be a game-changer, but if you give in to what can feel like natural, even justified defensiveness, that sense of safety can easily be disrupted. Second, know that being in service is as much about fostering this sense of understanding as it is about getting to solutions. Maybe there is no solution. As Maya Angelou, celebrated poet and author, once famously said:

I've learned that people will forget what you said, people will forget what you did, but people will never forget how you made them feel.

Matching service to need

Figure 9.2 illustrates the customized way you can serve based on the five reactions we've discussed.

Figure 9.2. Levels of Service Based on Identified Need

Serving the disengaged? Support them where they are. It may well be too late to save the disengaged from leaving, and for some, leaving is probably the best option anyway (recall Mike Candrea's story in Chapter 8 as a case in point). Your supporting that option can be tremendously healing to the relationship and the person. Consider the message it sends to someone when they feel seen as a person, not as merely a work commodity, and are supported to do what they think is best for them (as opposed to what the program or organisation wants).

Know, too, that if a bridge can be built to the disengaged, moving them back toward engagement becomes a possibility—but only when we lead with support. We hear where they are, we ask what they need. If a disengaged person is able to tell you what might help, it is incumbent upon you to be honest about what you can provide. And it goes without saying that you follow through on whatever support you agree to provide.

Serving the rigid? Provide perspective. Rigidity can come disguised as despondency or disengagement, but in the process of exploring with someone why they are "not right," you can often hear the undertones of anger and frustration that suggest the person is being overly reactive to the situation. Here, you give the person the space to articulate what they are angry about or what they think is unfair. This is another case of meeting them where they are before moving forward. It is obvious to everyone, often *including* the rigid person, that their emotional reaction to the situation is not getting them where they want to be. Rather, the sense of outrage that something is unfair or terrible has the tendency to hold a person frozen in place. So it's a matter of, in a psychic sense, standing beside them, looking out at what is outrageous, together. Yep, you get how that can feel awful and can see the perceived disparity in fairness. Yep, it sucks that we don't get to compete and train when and how we want. You can even empathise, if you feel similarly—all of this is an entirely human experience, after all. And then, you pivot back around to talk *to* the person. To convey both realities: Yep, it sucks. And how's the focusing on the suckiness treating you? How helpful is that for you? How is that line of thinking serving you right now?

Many a rigid person will want to hang on to their rigidity and anger; after all, these reactions can provide certainty and comfort, of a sort. But your ability to check in over and over about the pain this orientation is causing—without any resolution—can serve to let out some of the outraged air from a rigid person's tires. At the same time, you're pointing out the reality of the situation, what the future might hold (to the extent it is visible), as well as what might be more helpful right now. And rather than telling that to the person, ask: "How is that way of thinking helping you right now?" And listening with empathy to what comes from that. Keeping in mind that empathy, the ability to see things from the rigid person's perspective is not the same as agreeing with it. You are just making it safer, by conveying your understanding of their version of reality, to talk about it.

It's also about pointing out and questioning the underlying aspects that the rigid person is either gripping or pushing away. For example: "I'm angry because I hate uncertainty." OK, so what's so bad about uncertainty? Or "I'm pissed because I put all my planning eggs into a 2020 Olympics basket so I could retire, marry my sweetheart, and get on with life in 2021." OK, so what does it mean if you delay that? What will your life look like? Getting the rigid to actually talk about what they are afraid will happen, or with the goal of loosening their mental grip on the thing they believe *has* to happen, can be helpful in increasing their mental flexibility.

Serving the indecisive? Provide structure and reassurance. For overwhelmed people, simply offering some structure or asking them questions about how *they* might structure things can be helpful to put some boundaries around their thinking. For the truly overwhelmed, this can be as concrete as "What's next on your schedule after you leave my office? What about after that?" Co-building structure provides some security and is subtly empowering these individuals with the knowledge that, even when they are overwhelmed, they can come up with a "what to do next" plan. And then reassure, but only as long as you think their plan is reasonable. If not, then it might be necessary to go back to providing the structure. But to the extent you are able, co-create some structure and then reinforce their wisdom as it appears.

Serving the curious? Listen, reinforce, and provide counsel. For some people, moving from threat to possibility to opportunity is novel, while for others, it is second nature. It's the job of the coach and staff person to know who's who. For the constant innovator who always pushes boundaries, the counsel may be more measured. But in the case of the more cautious or pessimistic person, we want to be alert for when a shift happens so we can pick up on it and help expand ideas and fan the flame. When a person is able to pivot from threat and hypervigilance to curiosity, this is important—for mental health and well-being, if nothing else. We want to join in to understand their thinking, reinforce reasonable ideas, and tweak direction if needed.

And watch out for, as noted earlier, any of the more toxic "why" curiosity, and educate the person on its counterproductive ineffectiveness. Steer back to the more kind and open type of curiosity that promotes inquiry and learning.

Serving the engaged? Partner. This kind of interaction goes back to the psychic side-by-side form of interaction, as a way of checking in and looking to be effective for that person, over and over again. Reflecting back to Bronwen Knox's story and how she innovated her way into more playing roles—while having to work against the rigidity of her coaches—makes me wonder how much time and effort might have been spared, and what might have become of a less tenacious and self-believing athlete who might have given up and disengaged. Consider the alternative—how a different, more open response from coaches, from curious questioning to even an active partnering, could have taken that innovative idea—allowing engaged athletes to go after more roles and skills—to a whole new level. The likely result would have been a team with more skill, more agility, and more ability to handle uncertainties in the pool—and out.

In this chapter, I talked about the personal performance-enhancing values of enacting our purpose in the service of others, as well as some ways to individualize our service based on where those we serve may be—mentally and emotionally. In the next section, I get into the concept of effort, which arguably is where grit is most often on display, and where it can be a hero or a villain. I unpack some effort myths and get into the idea of "clean effort" as the way to harness and work with our gritty natures more effectively.

KEY TAKEAWAYS

✓ In times of uncertainty, when we move out of our own sense of fear and threat, or our own myopic self-focus, and lean into understanding the suffering of others in order to find a way to serve them where they are, we most certainly serve ourselves.

✓ To serve well requires an understanding of what service is required. This depends on how the people you seek to serve are reacting to the uncertainty.

✓ Common reactions to uncertainty include disengagement, rigidity, indecision/confusion, curiosity, and engagement.

✓ Each of these reactive tendencies requires a distinctly different service approach.
   ○ When serving the disengaged, provide support.
   ○ When serving the rigid, provide perspective.
   ○ When serving the indecisive, provide structure.
   ○ When serving the curious, provide counsel.
   ○ When serving the engaged, partner.

PART IV
INTRODUCTION TO EFFORT

In this book's final section, we go from theory to action. That is, we have learned about the qualities of grit, the times when those qualities work for us, and when and where they fail us. We have learned about how to hone our mindset to better suit our needs when life is tough, change is in the air, and uncertainty is legion. We have seen passion's limitations and learned how to craft and implement a more nimble and "made for purpose" purpose. As well, we have looked at how our purpose could be enacted in good service to ourselves and others. All good things to know, try, and implement in our lives.

But what about the "getting after it" bit? How can and should we take best action in times of change and uncertainty? This is where the concept of effort comes in. Effort is the mental or physical *activity* needed to *do* something. The definition is courtesy of the *Cambridge Dictionary*, but the italics are mine. They are there to illustrate a simple but compelling reality: that it is through our efforts—our behaviours—that our grit is on view for others. And it is through the viewing of others' efforts that we come to appreciate what grit looks like and start to differentiate between the truly gritty and the rest of us.

The point this section seeks to make is simple in the sense that, while effort is how we personify our grit, so to speak, not all efforts are created equal. Moreover, not all effort is good effort, and some efforts are true disasters in the sense that they are taking us in the wrong direction or actually hurting us. And sometimes, quitting is a far better option than continuing to exert effort harmfully or mindlessly.

- Chapter 10, "When Perseverance Goes Awry," outlines the common thinking errors we make in the interest of sticking to something too long, too far, or too much. Some efforts have an expiration date that we miss or ignore to our peril.

- Chapter 11, "The Case Against and For Quitting," cuts to the chase and debunks the societal mythology that suggests that "quitters never win and winners never quit" and outlines when quitting is actually in our best interest.

- Chapter 12, "Cleaning Up Effort," gets into the psychology of effort, how we tend to get into and can get out of our own way as we tackle those toughest of challenges. Doing hard things is hard enough. We can be easier and cleaner on the inside even as we "effort hard" on the outside.

10 WHEN PERSEVERANCE GOES AWRY

I n the grit self-assessment provided in Angela Duckworth's (2016) book, she intersperses statements reflective of grit's two underlying constructs: passion and perseverance. We've considered passion in Chapter 8; now let's take a closer look at the role of perseverance when grit is not enough. Here is Duckworth's list of statements suggestive of one's relative degree of perseverance:

- Setbacks don't discourage me. I don't give up easily.
- I am a hard worker.
- I finish whatever I begin.
- I am diligent. I never give up.
- I have overcome setbacks to conquer an important challenge. (p. 65)

On the one hand, who doesn't want to be this person? Interestingly, Duckworth notes that people who score high on grit overall tend to score relatively higher on the perseverance versus the passion side of the equation. That was certainly true for me. On the perseverance items, I scored 4 to 5 on the 5-point scale, while my sense of passion ranged from 2 to 5. As Duckworth notes, it's not just about *falling* in love with what you are doing; it's about *staying* in love (p. 64). So while I have loved deeply—taking my sport psychology career as an example—I have seen my passion for the work first flow and then ebb. But when I am in flow, during those times when my passion is at full-throttle, watch out.

If there's a common characteristic of gritty people (after all, our passions will be different and, as we have seen, may change over time), it's our tendency to put in the sustained effort—to persevere, to never give up when we have that passion or purpose bit between our teeth.

It is this characteristic, however, that is the leading problem for those who overindex on grit. We overwork our efforts. We wear out our perseverance. We continue to "dance with the one who brung us," as the saying goes, not realising that the dance party ended hours ago. Let's consider the ways that we may—intentionally or not—outstay effort's welcome to the detriment of our journey and ourselves.

When We Overstay Our Passion or Drift from Our Purpose

This error has a few different faces, all involving some version of a journey that began as one worth taking . . . until it was not anymore but we didn't realize it. This effort habit can be hard to identify for those who gain comfort and a sense of identity from their hard work. We like to work hard. We have always relied on this behaviour to get us where we want to go. And we persist in the thinking habit that suggests that where we are headed is where we want to go.

How do we know when our passion or purpose has in fact flown the coop? As was discussed in Section 2 on mindset, our ability to notice when something's not quite right is radically enhanced when we take the time to build up our self-awareness. The awareness I speak of is our ability to listen to, to be with and not fight or flee from the sense of discomfort or unease that emerges when we first become aware that things are not aligning. I find that many gritty people have actually learned to disregard their intuition or fear in the interest of just getting on with things.

The other way in which people hone this awareness is through a regular purpose check-in. Thinking back to Cindra Kamphoff's story in Chapter 8, this can be as simple as asking yourself questions like these: *Is this still what I want to be doing? Why? Does this give me energy or does it take it away? When I think of this pursuit, does it continue to make me happy? Does it still seem compelling?* And then listen to the answers that come back.

When We Mistake Activity for Achievement

Too often, we can burn ourselves out exerting effort on the wrong stuff, things that seem important or useful but in the end don't add value to the journey we are on. I fell into this trap often, doing lots of small things like painstakingly and personally answering all of my emails, which was very rewarding to me as it pushed both my "tick things off the list" button as well as my "be as nice to others as possible" button. I could also feel good about being industrious—another value I hold dear and I imagine is a sweet spot for many a Person of Grit. What I thought was a triple win, however, ended up eating up hours in my day.

Are there gritty processes that seem rewarding but are not getting you closer to where you want to go? Do you find yourself telling others how busy you are and lamenting the lack of time you have in your day?

What can you do about this? First, get clear around what "achievement" versus "activity" in your context means. I've been in workplaces where it was a source of pride to be seen as the first person in and the last to leave, as if performance was only about the number of hours you were present. In that kind of culture, it's easy to slide into thinking that time equals performance, when, in fact, it may have the opposite effect. Are you prone to giving yourself credit for time spent rather than what you were able to get done? I've seen this when athletes show up in body but not spirit to training—the slow walk into the gym, the lean onto the wall, the slow slide of butt to the floor, waiting for practice to start. The "get into the middle of the pack" mentality. Cruising, not engaging. Active but not achieving.

Second, are you working on the right stuff and then, by extension, not working on the wrong stuff? Another way to say this would be, if you were to define your true purpose or calling, are your actions limited to moving you toward that, and have you cut out the superfluous?

Angela Duckworth tells the story of Warren Buffett

(pp. 78–79), who taught a three-step process for career goal clarification:

1. Write down your top 25 career goals.
2. Circle your top 5.
3. Avoid doing anything related to the 20 goals you did not circle.

This approach may seem brutal, but it's a sound way to simplify your life and direct your effort to only that which is most important and therefore worth your limited time to do.

Personally, I have my own criteria I use to work out where to spend my effort and time:

1. Does this activity take me toward my purpose (i.e., build my business, love my family, be a good friend)?
2. Does it enhance or detract from my ability to do those things (build or undercut my mojo)?
3. Does it align with my core values (do good, be kind, be here)?

With these criteria in mind, I have, for example, reverse-engineered my day to do the things first thing in the morning that set me up best to tackle the rest of my day: exercise, get outside, meditate.

I worked with a very talented, dare I say headstrong, up-and-comer flatwater kayak athlete named Bob, tagged by his sport's coaches to be a legitimate contender for the Olympics. Moreover, in a sport that had both double and individual events, Bob was seen as having the take-no-prisoners attitude needed to be a singles kayaker, and my job was to continue the mental grooming toward this goal. Everything was moving along smoothly. Bob was hungry for anything that would hasten his trajectory and worked hard on, well, working hard. This was all well and good . . . until it wasn't.

Bob started to struggle in training for reasons no one could fathom. His times were slowing, he was starting to struggle with pain he'd not encountered before, his resting heart rate was elevating (a tell-tale sign of inadequate recovery), and his need for sleep was going through the roof. Initially, he was diagnosed with overtraining syndrome (a condition brought on by too much training without adequate recovery), but as months went by, this diagnosis was amended to a form of chronic fatigue, now known in the sport world as chronic overtraining syndrome.

In a matter of weeks, Bob went from *How hard can I go?* to *It can't be easy enough.* It was one thing to adapt to having a body that refused to obey you and quite another to cope with the self-concept U-turn and emotional fallout. Bob had truly lost his mojo and was pissed as hell about it.

Without a doubt, the first order of business was to enter into a deep and sustained physical recovery zone, but as important was the need for him to get easier in his thinking. For Bob, this meant loosening his hold on the unfairness of his predicament, of resisting the urge to ruminate on and lash out at his "lucky" teammates who were continuing to succeed without any of Bob's discipline or worth ethic.

This meant jettisoning the very mindset that got Bob to

this point and embracing the opposite: How can I go lighter, recover better, and make any efforts I put forth as easy as possible? Over a period of months, Bob gradually recovered, but the road back was pot-holed with setbacks fuelled by impatience. Bob eventually learned to rein in his frustration in favour of a gentler approach, and he came to credit this experience with making him more self-reflective and now more quickly responsive to what his body needed, not just what he wanted from it. In the end, he retired from sport, but he comforts himself knowing that his relationships to his body and mind are, due to this experience and the work he did, much better than they once were.

When We Mindlessly Refuse to Give Up

As part of a workshop I ran on the topic of inner high performance with a group of national team coaches, I asked them to speak to their understanding of and experience with grit. As soon as the word "grit" came out of my mouth, Mike Kohn, USA Bobsled coach, looked up with a wry grin and told this story about his epic battle with a lawnmower:

> My wife and I, we live in Myrtle Beach with our kids. We have a lawnmower, and the lawnmower had not been started in a while. And so I went in the garage and tried to start it, and it didn't start. My wife was in the garage; I think she was painting or something. So I started pulling on the cord, and it wouldn't start. And it was really hot, really hot in South Carolina—it was midsummer. And I kept yanking on it. She just kind of looked at me and smiled and

*looked back down and I looked at her and at that moment, I felt
like, "I have to start this lawnmower." It has to start because she
looked at me.*

*I think I may have been able to walk away at that point, but when
she looked at me, I felt like, "This is my wife; this is the woman I
love. I have to protect her at all costs. I got to get this lawnmower
started." And so I pulled on it. And I'm ripping on this thing. And I
felt this burning in my arm. You could probably see the bump right
there [gestures].*

*So I tore the muscle off of that right there and I pulled it as hard
as I could—burning like crazy and I didn't care—"I'm starting
this thing," and sure enough, I don't know how long it was, I think
probably 30 to 45 minutes, it finally started.*

Mike's own reaction to telling that story was one of sheepish
pride, as in "I know it was irrational and dumb, but that didn't
matter. Beating the mower was the important thing." I revisited
this conversation with Mike a few months later. He said that
upon reflection after he first told the story, his doggedness had
less to do with the lawnmower and more to do with the fact that
it was a period of downtime in his bobsled day job, and that
lawn care seemed like the way he could demonstrate that he
was fulfilling his responsibility to his family.

All this is not to say that there won't be some irrational
times for all of us, when just getting a job done no matter
what is the thing. I will argue, however, that we should cultivate an awareness of *why* we are doing what we are doing. I

appreciated Mike's honesty and awareness around his need to start a lawnmower being about much more than that—it was really about feeling useful. Good to know.

As important, however, it would be useful to know when to *stop* doing that thing in the interest of our physical and mental health. A case in point: There no longer exists a World Sauna Championship. An annual event held in Heinola, Finland, from 1999 to 2010, it was cancelled after one of the two finalists died from burns and trauma from the extreme heat, while the other was hospitalized, having refused to leave the sauna after appearing to be sick.

The BBC ("Finalist Dies," 2010) reported this response from Ossi Arvela, the event's chief organizer:

> All the rules were followed and there were enough first aid personnel. All the competitors needed to sign in to the competition with a doctor's certificate. Half a litre of water was added to the stove inside the sauna every 30 seconds, and the last person remaining was the winner.

Event medical staff also checked in periodically with participants, with both finalists asserting their fitness to continue, giving the required "thumbs-up" at every point . . . until it became clear that they were not. So it turns out that our will can find a way around even those protections meant to save us from ourselves.

On April 20, 2011, the City of Heinola ("The Future," n.d.) announced that they would no longer organise the event, noting,

If the city was to organize the World Sauna Championships in
*the future, the **original playful and joyous characteristics of the***
***event** should be reintroduced. No ways to achieve this have been*
found. (emphasis added)

I am intrigued to know more about what sauna-goers find
playful and joyous in this activity, but I could not agree more
that this intended spirit of the event was corrupted somewhere along the way. There's an important lesson here about
the process versus the product inherent in any challenge.
That is, sometimes when we persevere toward our goal to our
own detriment—thus mucking up our processes—we can do
more harm than good and wind up farther from our goal than
nearer to it.

This story begs the question of whether, once that happens and we have lost our way in our journey, we can do a
reset of our processes to get back to our original purpose. It
is interesting to read of the World Sauna Championship event
organisers' own pessimism around recapturing that spirit.
Perhaps it was a matter, in this case, of participant deaths
being a "bridge too far." The severity of the price paid for going
beyond that tipping point of a fun, challenging, culturally
significant activity into profound suffering and death was just
too much to bear, frankly, too traumatic for anyone to imagine
continuing. I don't think too many of us would argue that, in
this case, it really was the best and, frankly, the only choice
to cease and desist. Fun and challenge had been usurped by
trauma and death.

For the rest of us in the midst of our own gritty journeys, these kinds of choices—to persevere or step away—will not be as obvious or clear as what confronted the town of Heinola and their now-defunct championships. At least let us all hope that our journeys don't lead us to those kinds of outcomes. But what I have noticed with the über-gritty is that the idea of quitting something—anything—is not only not obvious, but seen as verboten and unthinkable.

In the interest of making the unthinkable at least thinkable, the next chapter, "The Case Against and For Quitting," confronts the sometimes-controversial concept of quitting—why we hate to do it, when it's just giving up, and when the smart quit can be in our very best interest.

KEY TAKEAWAYS

✓ People who score high on grit overall tend to score relatively higher on the perseverance versus the passion side of the equation.

✓ It is the perseverance characteristic that is the leading problem for those who overindex on grit. We overwork our efforts. We wear out our perseverance.

✓ Common reasons for this overgritting tendency include lacking self-awareness, mistaking activity for achievement, confusing time spent with outcomes achieved, and mindlessly refusing to give up.

11 THE CASE AGAINST AND FOR QUITTING

I f there is a word that high achievers, especially those who pride themselves on their grit, hate more than any other, it would be *quit*. And if there were two words to hate, they'd be *give up*. The book *Grit* rests firmly on the premise that getting to that place of achievement is the most important thing. The insight Angela Duckworth delivered was that to do this takes more than "just" talent and that those other things (passion and perseverance) are actually more important. There's the recipe, people! If you want to cross that Important Long-Term Challenge finish line, get gritty. In this version of reality—finishing what you start—quitting is the opposite of grit.

Having talked to Duckworth about this, and knowing her personal career story, which has its share of twists and turns, I know she is not advocating never quitting but rather staying true and continuing to persevere toward one's longer-term passion or vision as it matures. I believe, however, that this kind of nuance is lost in favour of the old chestnut "Quitters never win and winners never quit." Moral certitude feels so much better!

In this chapter, we'll look at what circumstances may warrant—dare I say it—giving up on a challenge, no matter how much grit, passion, and perseverance we can manifest.

Why We Hate to Quit

Quitting has become, in certain circles, akin to a moral failing—that is, if it isn't already a sign of some larger societal failure. We struggle with quitters but love a good rags-to-riches perseverance saga.

How many stories have we heard about the successful, gritty person whose life story began when a (hopefully but not always) well-meaning parent or teacher told them they weren't good enough to reach their dreams, thus inspiring the person to double down in an "I'll show you!" kind of way and achieve success? Think of Walt Disney, who as a newspaper writer persisted despite being fired from his job at the *Kansas City Star* for not being creative enough. Think of Thomas Edison, who was told by his teachers that he was "too stupid to learn anything," was fired from his first two jobs for not being productive enough, and famously failed 2,000 times in trying to find an effective filament for his lightbulb. These stories live on in our collective consciousness, inspiring us to believe that quitting is not for winners or the truly successful.

Another reason we hate quitting is our often irrational view of loss. Imagine this scenario: You are walking down the street and find a $10 bill. You put the money into your wallet. A day later, you go to buy a coffee with that money, but the bill has disappeared. Which emotion, the pleasure of the find or the disappointment of the loss, is greater? Psychologists Daniel Kahneman and Amos Tversky (1979) coined the term "loss aversion" to describe the results of their research that suggest that our aversion to loss is *twice* as strong as our pleasure in gain. When we view quitting through this psychological lens, it isn't hard to see how people can become more focused on the pain of what they are losing.

Steven Dubner (2011), in an episode of his *Freakonomics* podcast called "The Upside of Quitting," extends this argument, invoking the idea of the "sunk cost fallacy" and its impact on our views on quitting. The sunk cost fallacy is the tendency we have to make future decisions based on the investment we have already made in something, even if doing so is no longer the best decision or in our current best interest. An example of this is when a person buys a restaurant meal and overeats "just to get my money's worth." This thinking also can make people overly hesitant to quit a job or change careers based in part on their past investment in training or education. Dubner suggests that we're so loss-averse that we favour sunk cost over an equally important consideration: opportunity cost. For every hour or dollar that you spend on one thing, you're giving up the opportunity to spend that hour or dollar on something else, "something that might make your life better—if only you weren't so worried about the sunk cost," he says.

Quitting Is, Well, Complicated

As we have seen, there are factors ranging from our basic psychology to our cultural conditioning that have conspired to make the idea of quitting quite unpalatable for many of us, sometimes to our detriment. Yet, intuitively, we also know that there are times when we have to stop something in order to start something better, or when the thing we are doing is not good for us. So how do we get this decision right more often?

When quitting is the right thing to do

The unsurprising yet unsatisfying short answer to the question "When is quitting the right thing to do?" is "It depends." It depends on how old you are. That is, children have little experience to use as context from which to judge the quality of an experience and therefore can and do quit things for all sorts of reasons—some of them invalid. Parents are often counselled, therefore, to set some boundaries on quitting, such as telling their children that they can freely choose to start an activity, a sport, or a hobby but must persevere with it for a minimal period of time, say a sport season, so as to learn to persevere over momentary difficulty, boredom, or disinterest. Angela Duckworth's family, for example, live by the Hard Thing Rule. Everyone in the family, parents included, has to engage in one hard thing that requires daily practice. You can quit your hard thing, but only when there's a natural stopping point, not because it got hard one day. And, finally, if you quit, you find another Hard Thing to replace it.

Whether and when to quit also depends on your perspective on effort and time. We are more likely to steer away from short-term pain than to focus effectively on the longer-term benefits in so many endeavours. This is why diets and New Year's resolutions so often fail. The inspiration of achieving that Big

Goal is alluring enough to get us started, but the cumulative pain brought on by deprivation or effortful behaviour pulls us back to our status quo. There is many a cottage industry built up to help us in this space—trainers, personal coaches, and more. The bottom line goes back to Duckworth's Hard Thing Rule: don't quit something with good long-term potential just because you are stressed, anxious, overwhelmed, or [fill in the blank here with your preferred painful-experience adjective].

To that end, I will ask demotivated athletes to draw a picture of a mountain—with themselves on the side of it (see Figure 11.1 for an example)—and then label the top with whatever their current Big Goal is. We then use the side of the mountain as a sort of achievement timeline, with the assignment being to have as many achievements underneath the stick figure as short-term goals above it. While athletes invariably chafe against this assignment to start, it can renew hope and refresh a sense of greater perspective on the journey that is nearly always useful. For it is very common to only look up the mountain and feel demotivated at all there is still to climb—without a periodic backward glance at how far they have come. Alternatively, this process can make clear what's required—and act as the wake-up call to change course or, in some instances, even stop the climb.

What perhaps not to do when you quit

Related to this, we have all had situations where we have felt hard done by and become overcome with frustration, grief, disappointment, or other negative emotions. As I write this book, the 2020 year-delayed Olympics have just concluded.

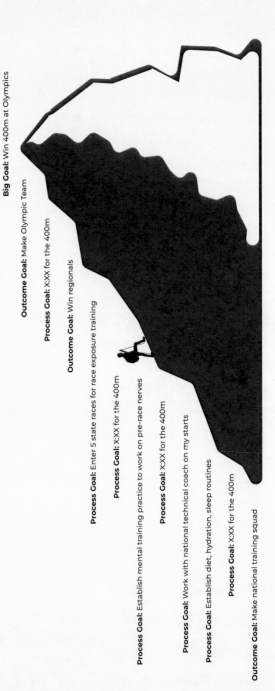

Big Goal: Win 400m at Olympics

Outcome Goal: Make Olympic Team

Process Goal: X:XX for the 400m

Outcome Goal: Win regionals

Process Goal: Enter 5 state races for race exposure training

Process Goal: X:XX for the 400m

Process Goal: Establish mental training practice to work on pre-race nerves

Process Goal: X:XX for the 400m

Process Goal: Work with national technical coach on my starts

Process Goal: Establish diet, hydration, sleep routines

Process Goal: X:XX for the 400m

Outcome Goal: Make national training squad

Figure 11.1. Process and Outcome Goal Timeline Example

For every grateful and excited medallist, there are many more athletes who either lost out during the selection process or did not have the Games they had hoped for. As tempting as it might be, when you have had it "up to here" with your coach, the selection process, your teammates, or your sport's high-performance director, and think you will go out in a blaze of "let 'em have it" glory, think again. Rather than giving in to the short-term satisfaction of the bombshell exit, I ask athletes to consider their legacy with a long-term view. How do you want to remember and be remembered as an athlete and by your sport? Maybe you come to the same conclusion but do so with eyes wide open to both the gain and the loss potentially inherent for you. They don't call this kind of quitting "burning your bridges" for nothing.

> Bronwen Knox, the water polo athlete we first heard from in Chapter 9, tells the story about timing her quit. In the lead-up to the 2016 Olympics, dynamics on the Australian team were particularly fraught, and Bronwen's role as team leader was regularly undermined by the coaching staff. She realised she'd lost her sport mojo and toyed with the idea of quitting. While she could have made a louder statement calling out the subpar team status quo by timing her quit to happen pre-Games, Knox was acutely aware of what that would do to her teammates who she knew were also struggling. Knox set aside her own difficulties and continued to perform for her team, but once the Games were over, she announced that she was taking a break from the sport. Stepping away was the best decision she could have made, Knox acknowledged. "It gave me time to do some other things that

needed doing in my life, and this way, I had the option to return if
things changed and my love of the sport came back." And come
back it did. Knox returned for a final fourth Olympics in Tokyo, a
decision she is glad she made.

When quitting is the smart thing to do

The answer to the question "When is quitting the smart thing to do?" is "More often than we gritty folk might think." It turns out that successful people in any domain are really good at sussing out the wheat from the chaff in any endeavour—and quitting both fast and lightly those things that are not serving them. "Failing fast" has become a popular catch phrase, especially in companies like Apple and SharkNinja, that want their employees to stretch their creativity and brainpower to generate novel ideas, try them out with product teams who make facsimiles to manifest the ideas, and then see what happens. If those ideas work, great—the next iteration of a smartphone is born. If not, it's not a big deal and the team goes on to the next brainstorming/idea-testing session.

Doing this well, however, starts with having a clear picture of yourself and what's important. Too many of us hold onto, without really realising it, outmoded ideas about who we are and where we really want to go.

I facilitated a day-long workshop for a group of executives around the idea that if you wanted to be a high performer, you had to care for yourself first and then dive into what that looked like for you the individual, your relationships, and your work. A follow-up event after the workshop involved a behaviour-change challenge. Participants were encouraged to experiment with making one lifestyle change and report the result of their efforts—good, bad, or ugly—back to the group during our follow-up time together.

One participant blew us all away with his story about how just the idea of making a single behaviour change was enough to get him reflecting on his life as a whole, how many good things he had let fall by the wayside over the past months, and, frankly, how miserable he had become. These insights fuelled his decision to take a six-month leave of absence from his job to "get my life back in order. I miss doing the things that give me joy, such as playing the flute and volunteering. What I can't figure out is how I ever allowed this to happen in the first place!"

What this example speaks to is the importance of per-forming regular check-ins on your own journey. Just because something was the absolute right thing to do a while back doesn't necessarily mean it still applies today.

Quitting More Efficiently

Even as we may become intellectually aware that our long-term goals are no longer fit for purpose, we often prevaricate on quitting. If we are not careful, however, we pay a price for this indecision. While sticking with it rather than making the decision to quit can look strong to others (or so we might think), what the story above suggests is that we pay a price for that indecision. I once worked for a wonderful boss but also a king of clutter who had an acronym taped over his desk:

EPPIADU, for "Every piece of paper is a decision unmade." This idea has always stuck with me. We may think that we can afford to prevaricate on decisions—that the piece of paper represents the possibility of a better decision, or that we just can't be bothered to decide this instant—but it's a trap. Our minds become as cluttered as my old boss's desk.

Seth Godin (2007), in his fiery little book *The Dip*, has three questions for people who are wondering if quitting is the answer. Spoiler alert: *The Dip* exposes both the virtues and downsides of quitting, suggesting that too many of us quit too early and for the wrong reasons, while others suffer from not quitting fast enough, wasting valuable time doing mediocre work. Here are the three questions:

1. Are you panicking? Panicking is not premeditated and almost always leads to bad decisions. Godin suggests instead that we pre-decide when quitting is the go-to move or, as he says, quit before we start. That is, what would be the conditions where you would consider quitting? Godin quotes ultramarathoner Doug Collins, who said, "Decide before the race the conditions that would cause you to stop and drop out. You don't want to be out there saying, 'Well, gee, my leg hurts, I'm a little dehydrated, I'm sleepy, I'm tired, and it's cold and windy.' And talk yourself into quitting. If you are making a decision based on how you are feeling in that moment, you will probably make the wrong decision."

2. At what level are you trying to influence? Sometimes we can't see the forest for the trees—for example, getting frustrated with one person as opposed to zooming out and considering the whole of your relationships. If you are trying to influence or work better with one person, there's only so much you can do, but when you can de-emphasize that particular relationship in favour of how you are working with the greater group, there's generally more leeway because different people in the group think differently. Even if a few have closed their minds to you, it is rare that all will.

3. What sort of measurable progress are you making?

Getting through tough times on any journey means accessing your progress points regularly. And Godin is clear: if progress is not happening, then quitting's the answer. My experience with elite athletes suggests to me that most have an aversion to resting on their laurels and a drive to get to the Next Thing. This attitude makes for an active lifestyle, but it also can create a bias against seeing progress since all they see is how far they have yet to go (remember Figure 11.1?). Stopping to measure progress is important for motivational reasons, but more important, it's the data you need to determine if it's worth persisting—or trying something else.

In the case of quitting something like a job or a big task, the clutter is just "louder," since the decision feels all the more important. Make your prevarications count by going beyond the worry loops and indecision and actually answering the questions your doubts are asking. Consider the consequences of quitting, not just from the perspectives of what you stand to lose or gain but also, hearkening back to Seth Godin, by asking yourself, "If I quit this task, will it increase my ability to get through my dip and on to something more important?" Above all, know that a good quit is transformed into a great quit when you waste less time prevaricating ineffectively about it and get on with it.

Learning from Your Quits

David Epstein's (2019) book *Range* argues that starting a specialised path early and doggedly sticking to it is for most of us not as smart as sampling early and often and quitting what is unfulfilling or otherwise a bad match. Borrowing a term from economists, Epstein calls this process one of determining "match quality." Especially for young people with less life experience, sampling and quitting ramps up one's self-knowledge exponentially faster than persisting, especially if persistence means remaining in an unhappy job or career.

The key is *learning* from your quitting. Ask yourself, "What made this a bad match, or, what match qualities were missing?" In their haste to get out of what is perceived as a bad situation (otherwise, why quit?), or because reflecting on one's perceived failure is too painful ("Ouch, I quit—let's just turn that page ASAP"), too many quitters don't take the time to ask this question, much less answer it.

In seeking answers to that question, prepare to go beneath the easy, superficial, or "answers as excuses" responses, as in, "I just wasn't happy," "My coach was a jerk," or "I'd have been great if so-and-so offered more support." Any or all of these might be true, but none of them inform you going forward. These are less answers and more ego-preserving observations and rationalisa-tions. Using marriage as a metaphor here, the relationship for good or bad should be considered a dance between two people. When a marriage ends, it's rarely just one person's fault. So if I quit something—it could be a job, a quest, or a relationship—it can be useful to consider an amicable dissolution—just as mari-tal therapists suggest for couples who can't reconcile. Embedded in that is the understanding of how each partner contributed to and subtracted from the relationship. And from that under-standing, considering how I will want to do better next time.

In the case of you and your quit, here are some areas to focus on and questions to consider.

Environmental/Contextual

Was there anything in the context of your situation that made things easier or harder than they had to be? While this could be something as simple or as obvious as, say, a long com-mute, in the context of a relationship, it could be the overbear-ing in-laws whose interference undermined the relationship. In a job, it could be that you realized that you're not cut out to be part of a team—or vice versa: that you need to be with other people doing the same thing. It's also useful to consider what you liked about the situation you were in—those aspects of the situation that you valued, that gave you energy, that you loved.

Relationships/Social Support

Were the people involved a help or a hindrance to your suc-cess or happiness in this venture, and if so, how? Get specific here. Go beyond the "My coach was a jerk" kind of sentiment to explore what, exactly, were the qualities or behaviours that were offensive to you? Virtually everything we do involves other people in some way, and understanding how and why we click with some personalities and not others can be a real game changer.

Personally, I have learned that I am very people-oriented and am heavily influenced—for good or bad—by those around me. To put it bluntly, I don't just need social support; I require a social safety net in the form of a solid and available professional and personal community from which to draw. And I have always loved working on a team of good people doing good work together. But supporting the notion that we are always changing, I have been nothing short of shocked to find that transitioning to working for myself has been immensely satisfying. I love creating my own way *and* knowing I have support to call in when I need it. Having said that, not all social support is equal, in my book. I don't respond to people who can't manage their emotions or who I see treating others unfairly (even if it's not happening to me).

Personal

Ask yourself, "How did I contribute to the problem? Is there a disconnect between who I know myself to be—my values— and what is valued in this situation?" This aspect of things can often be the most uncomfortable to address, given that it forces us to recognize our own limitations and failings. The answers to these questions may not reveal themselves, at least not without help, while we are in the quit process. Sometimes we are just too close to the fray and our egos are too invested.

Often, it is only after the fractious split has concluded and the emotional dust has settled that the participants can turn the mirror of relationship self-examination upon themselves.

Jane, a coaching client I worked with, came to see me initially because she had been repeatedly unable to pass her field's qualifying exam. Now, with her back against the wall, facing a "strike three" failure that would force her out of her field of choice, Jane was determined to grit her way to exam success while not alienating her family in the process. We worked for several sessions on the performance aspects of this journey, including how to help her family better integrate into her efforts as her "support team."

All was going to plan until we started explore in more depth her lack of motivation for study. It was here that Jane came up against the reality that, in the event that she passed her exam, the life she was signing up for—good pay but long hours and a grinding schedule—went against what she realized was an equal passion, being a mother to her three children. After more discussion, she decided to quit—not the profession, but the speciality—and transition into one with a lifestyle more in line with her values.

It is in coming to these honest answers, as Jane did, that we learn the most about ourselves and can move more intentionally to our own "next, best thing." And what we learn doesn't necessarily have to be painful but can be vastly, and importantly, informative. It is often said that we choose to do things, especially at the beginning of our lives or careers, with the smallest amount of life experience data, so no wonder we don't always get it right!

A way to structure this post-quit assessment is to create a help/hinder matrix for each area of inquiry (see Figure 11.2). This is a process I have used often, both with coaches and athletes, to help them make sense, post-event, of what worked well and what didn't, or what made the person/team go faster or get better versus what slowed them down or made them less effective. It can also be used as a way to systematically assess a situation pre-quit.

In this chapter, we reviewed the reasons why quitting is anathema to the gritty, as well as how this distaste, if applied too liberally, flies in the face of the evidence that suggests the smart quit is not only a hallmark of the truly successful but can help get you to success more quickly. We also unpacked what the process of the smart quit—a process that increases the chances of your "next thing" being more likely to succeed—can look like.

In the next, concluding chapter, we dig into the idea of effort quality. For those who identify as gritty, our efforts become the personification of who we are. But if our efforts are clouded, mistimed, or wrongly placed, we are either working harder than we need to or, worse, working hard on the wrong stuff. The chapter closes by contrasting these misguided uses of our grit (a finite resource, might I add) with how to "effort clean" with less cost and greater impact.

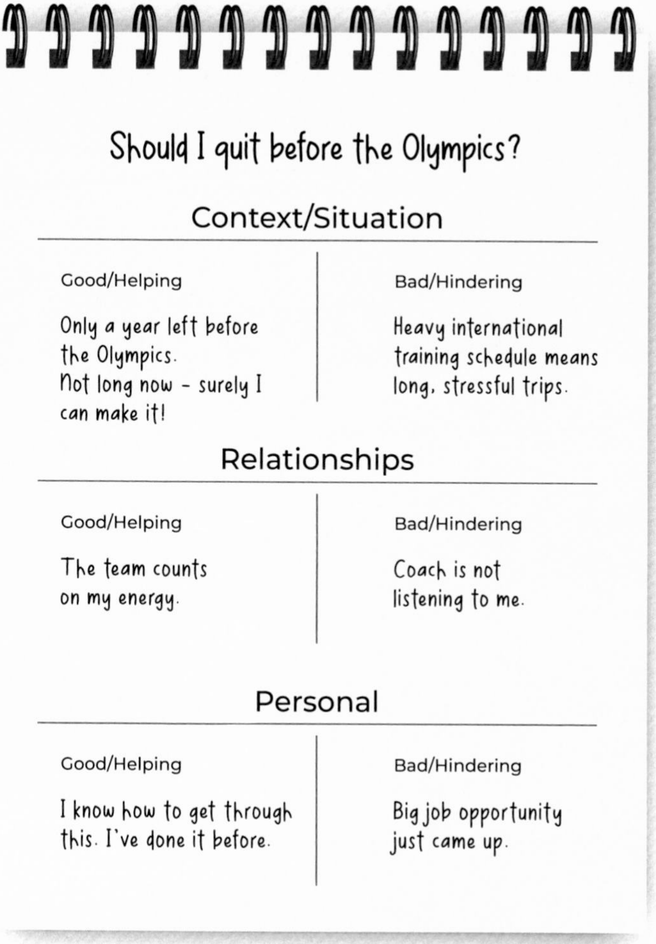

Should I quit before the Olympics?

Context/Situation

Good/Helping

Only a year left before
the Olympics.
Not long now – surely I
can make it!

Bad/Hindering

Heavy international
training schedule means
long, stressful trips.

Relationships

Good/Helping

The team counts
on my energy.

Bad/Hindering

Coach is not
listening to me.

Personal

Good/Helping

I know how to get through
this. I've done it before.

Bad/Hindering

Big job opportunity
just came up.

Figure 11.2. Help/Hinder Matrix

KEY TAKEAWAYS

✓ Gritty people tend to hate the idea of quitting, yet this rigidity is often the reason why grit can get us into trouble if, in fact, quitting is the smartest option.

✓ Our dislike of quitting is both culturally conditioned and the result of cognitive biases such as our outsized aversion to loss and the "sunk-cost" fallacy, the idea that once we have made an investment in something, we are loathe to give up on that investment even when it's in our best interest to do so.

✓ The decision to quit is complex because it is dependent on many situationally specific factors including age, the task at hand, how important the outcome is, and our quitting versus sticking history, to name a few variables.

✓ Whatever the reason for quitting, it's counterproductive to do so in a way that burns your bridges behind you.

✓ Getting good at smart quitting—knowing more quickly when quitting is the smartest play—starts with having a clear picture of yourself and what's important. Too many of us hold onto, without really realising it, outmoded ideas about who we are and where we really want to go.

- ✓ Seth Godin's three questions to ask in the face of a potential quit:
  - ○ **Are you panicking?** Don't decide anything in that state.
  - ○ **At what level are you trying to influence?** Sometimes the act of zooming out can give clarity to a too-small focus.
  - ○ **What sort of measurable progress are you making?** If you aren't moving, then quitting is often the best move.

- ✓ Never forget to learn from your quits. This keeps you from making the same mistakes over and over. Ask yourself, "What made this a bad match, or what match qualities were missing?"

12 CLEANING UP EFFORT

"**A**re we having fun yet?" This question from our teacher drew a few grim smiles and a grunt or two from the audience. I was in spin class, along with the familiar cohort of other die-hard early-morning exercisers, all pedalling madly to nowhere in a dark room with loud music pounding away in the background.

Normally I don't listen much to instructor banter, but this question got me thinking. I know it was meant as a joke—the presumption being that "fun" was not at all synonymous with our experience at that moment. And I bought into the sarcasm. The actual experience was not fun, exactly, but at the same time, I was aware that it was something very interesting, even compelling, to me.

How we perceive challenges is worth unpacking as we explore ways to make our own high-performance challenges less painful and build our grit. In this chapter, we will focus on physical challenges, but the strategies discussed here can easily apply to other kinds of challenges as well—say, handling the stresses of working from home, studying for exams, or anticipating a difficult performance-management conversation.

At issue here is that not all effort is created equal. We

can see that from the physical perspective—the person who "leaves it all on the line" versus the person who doesn't. What this chapter looks at are the mental underpinnings that make our hard efforts more difficult and what we can do about this. When our minds make our efforts harder than they have to be, that's dirty effort. Just as impure fuel hurts an engine over time, our dirty efforts can get the job done but can exact a cost on the operator (that's us). When, in contrast, our minds work together with the challenges on offer, our efforts can become cleaner, feel easier, and we can sustain them for longer periods of time.

Learning Firsthand About Effort

I was not always as willing to lean into the challenge of hard effort. What I was willing to do was to figure out how to put myself in the position to do the things I really wanted to do, which, it turns out, is not the same thing as doing them.

When I found out, back in the early 1980s, that there was a job called "sport psychologist," I was dead set on the idea of becoming one. I wrote to every program and person I found that was in some way related to this field. I sent letters, waited for responses, wrote some more, and waited some more. Sure enough, after several months, I had located a few programs, applied, and eventually got myself admitted to the University of Illinois. Check that box.

Then the cold, hard reality of graduate school hit me. Who was I to think I would survive advanced education? I became almost paralysed with anxiety, was sure I would fail, and almost talked myself into quitting. I did not think I could do the work.

The coping strategy I stumbled upon was brutal but effective: I got up very early each morning and went for a run. Running is funny in that it's easy to do—just one step after another—but becomes hard the longer you go. For me, it was often both a mental and a physical battle to finish.

But afterward, two things happened. First, it turns out endorphins are a thing—those post-exercise feel-good neurochemicals that kick in after significant physical efforts. I always finished feeling great. And second, I literally thought, "Surely nothing grad school can throw at me will hurt more than that!" And I was right.

The problem was that, as I got fitter, endorphins became harder to come by with the same effort. I had to run farther for the same positive effects. It also turned out that I was a sucker for a challenge independent of the feel-good effect. By the end of my first year of graduate school, I had signed up for and run my first marathon, which jump-started decades of regular running challenges, in part to remind me what challenge really felt like. I recently experienced this mental boost again by pinkie-swearing with a friend to run the New York Marathon together when we're 65!

Along the way in grad school, I became a student of my own mind under duress. I learned that what I *thought* about a challenge was more predictive of my ability to weather the challenge than the challenge itself. As a sport psychologist, I was "let into" the minds of average to elite athletes and coaches, and I saw how they did it. And as a mindfulness-meditation student and instructor, I have learned still more about the mind's responses to challenge and how to work with those. Here's what I learned along the way.

Not Believing Everything You See

The biggest "clean effort" insight for me, as a sport psychologist, was recognizing that what represents on the outside, to the casual observer of effort, is and should not be overinterpreted as what happens on the inside. Consider the swan that appears serene, majestic, and unruffled above water, until you look underneath and see how fast and furiously its feet are paddling. Because the mental side of things is unfortunately but inevitably invisible, people draw conclusions from what they can see. Whether it's from watching sport, viewing action movies, or even giving birth, we have seen the faces of people trying really hard to achieve some difficult goal: gritting their teeth, the veins in their neck standing out; and, of course, we think this must be what their minds are also doing: making an effort, exerting, punishing, driving.

Intense physical effort can make us appear (and feel) strained, but in our minds, if we are bringing our best mental game to our efforts, *less is more.* Clean effort in this instance means being in touch with reality as it is, facing, without reactivity, the sensations of fatigue and pain with an even keel and a sense of detached curiosity. Pain is still pain, no doubt about it; but when we are able to strip away the stories our minds are telling us—no, screaming at us—we start to recognize the nuances for what they are: strong sensations that never last forever, that ebb and flow.

I could well imagine that the term *mental toughness* is a product of this misunderstanding. Effort as seen from the outside looks to be all about toughness. Unfortunately, this concept has been misunderstood and weaponized over time, falsely equating the necessary physical manifestations of effort with how it must be in the mind. If your mind was "tough," you'd persevere through hard efforts. Therefore, when the individual failed in some way on the physical stage, it must be due to a flaw—a lack of toughness in their minds.

Everyone puts out effort, but not all efforts are created equal. Another way to look at it is that working hard is not always working smart. I call those hard efforts that don't get us places—or equally, the efforts that so seriously deplete us that we wonder if they were worth the effort—"dirty efforts." Yep, you've arrived at your destination, but was it worth it? Or worse, you burned out on the way there.

The goal, if we are honest about it, would be the greatest gains for the least effort. I call this kind of thinking and doing "clean effort." The flame of intent burns hot and bright, not smoky and diffuse. The spin instructor who informs the class, "Whoo boy, wait 'til you see what's coming next! You're going to hate this!" has just dirtied their efforts. Participants have to grapple with the possibility of hate, of doubt: *If the instructor thinks that, maybe it will be too hard for me.* The elite athlete who peppers her self-talk with name-calling and character assassination has to first recover from the self-inflicted onslaught before moving on. Those are just some examples of efforts that have been made (in my view) unnecessarily dirty.

How do we to get cleaner effort? Here are some ideas.

Cutting the Challenge Down to Size (but No Further)

Rather than the enemy being today's speedwork training plan, the spin bike, the big presentation, or that important exam, the enemy of effort very often is us. For example, as soon as I hear someone telling me how much they "hate" some particular workout or effort, I know there's a problem. Don't waste your effort energy in this way. Because that's what it is—a use of your finite emotional resources on something that does not care if you hate it or not. This reminds me of something Mark Twain reportedly said:

 Holding on to hate is like taking poison but hoping someone else will die.

The workout just *is*. Hating it hurts only you, even though it seems to feel good in the moment to express it. Instead, spend your finite resources focusing on what you need to do physically and mentally to prepare for and execute the workout. That is, can you imagine what the efforts will be and then devise strategies to meet them? For example, if you've got a recurring injury you fear might flare up during a jog, maybe you run slower, or for a shorter distance, or intersperse your run with walking. In addition, have you *accurately* imagined the discomfort/pain? Predicting the obvious—without cata-strophizing or minimizing it—is far better than being blind-sided by it.

Rower Scott Brennan framed up his ability to keep an uncluttered mind during high effort as a distinct competi-tive advantage:

> If one person is wasting their energy fighting this shit and it doesn't even register as something to be considered in the other person, who do you think is better off? You've got a task to perform that's already hard. It has technical demands, physical demands; it's got mental demands. You have a finite amount of energy. Do you want to spend it fighting these judgments that you have made? "This is hard, so now I have to be tough, and to be tough, I have to fight this and deny this pain—is it pain?—I'm calling it pain and I have to fight it"...

> Whereas the other person says, "This is causing some met-abolic noise. I just need to focus on what actually matters." Automatically, they are not wasting energy trying to negate something that they already understood. That if I want to do this task, this sensation [pain] is part of it. And why would I try to suppress something that is integral to what I am doing? Why am I wasting my energy—my finite energy—on something that actually cannot be removed from it? And this is what I don't understand—it's such a kind of pallid version of what tough should really be. You're biting [on] something when the ultimate toughness is that it doesn't even register. It may register, but

it doesn't draw a reaction out of you. I think that's probably the key. And why would you fight the thing you are doing? You know it—why fight it? Crazy.

At the same time, we do ourselves no favours trying to minimise or deny the likely impact of a tough physical challenge. Saying "It will be fine" when you don't actually know if it will be is just a setup to be blindsided, unprepared, and planless. Hope, as they say, is not a plan.

Classic sport psychology research (Rotella et al., 1980) put skiers faced with a challenge into two groups. The first group was to simply psych themselves up, telling themselves things like "I got this!" or "Keep trying!" The second group was instructed to combine positive self-talk with productive self-talk, with instructions such as "Keep those legs moving like pistons!" or "Breathe deep and push!" Turns out that positivity alone is not as effective as when it is paired with instruction about specifically what to do to deal with the challenge at hand.

Soothing the Brain with Nonreactivity

This strategy is a counter-intuitive one, but stay with me. Our brains are hard-wired to detect threat. As we learned in Chapter 3, this capability is in large part what helped us to survive as a species. Moreover, our brains are great at creating habit patterns—strengthening the neural networks of thought we use most often, so we don't even have to think about things as much. This is the "muscle memory" that eventually enables us to nail a perfect topspin backhand or land a triple axel without thinking twice. It's handy in some cases, but not always.

The reality is that physical challenge almost inevitably includes some pain. Not only does the brain hate pain, but it will bias toward habit formation that nips pain in the bud. Every athlete on the planet, if they want to get good at their endeavour of choice, has had to learn how to override the brain's tendency to scream "Stop!" at the first sign of pain. The journey to being elite is, then, a matter of continuing to hone one's pain discernment, balancing the need to push the pain envelope without overdoing into injury.

Cultivating the skill of nonreactivity is a superpower when it comes to these pain evaluations. The ability to evaluate without knee-jerk emotional judgments side-steps the futility of pretending pain doesn't exist by doing the opposite. As pain is perceived, first, just calmly notice it as accurately as possible. Literally, what does it feel like, and where in the body do I feel it?

Here, we are employing the same technique in how we view pain as we did regarding the workout itself. Rather than wasting precious mental resources focusing on how much we dislike the pain, fear the pain, or wish the pain would go away, we just let pain be as it is. Recognize that when we give into negative emotion-laden judgments like these about the pain, our evolutionary instinct for survival just won out over our intellectual understanding that the pain of hard effort will not kill us (unless, of course, we have a serious underlying medical weakness).

To illustrate these points, the two following figures

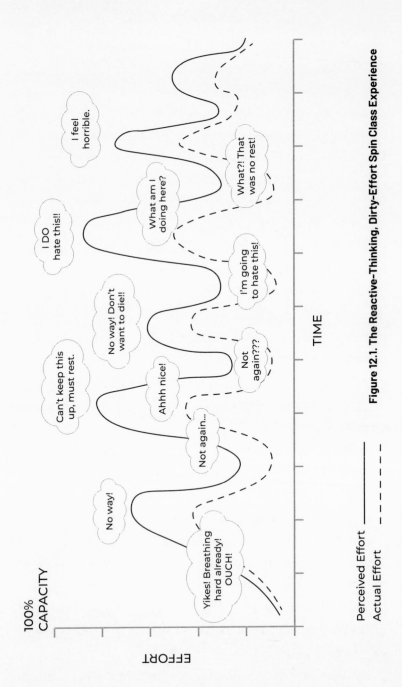

Figure 12.1. The Reactive-Thinking, Dirty-Effort Spin Class Experience

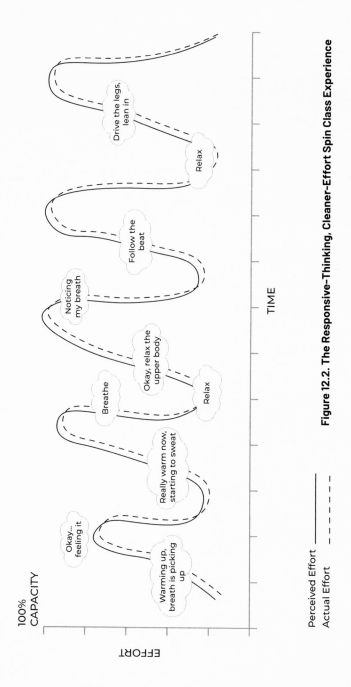

Figure 12.2. The Responsive-Thinking, Cleaner-Effort Spin Class Experience

illustrate the contrasting thinking and effort experiences of two spin cyclists, one of whom is reactive, the other responsive (as in simply responding to the demands of the workout).

Figure 12.1 illustrates the experience of the reactive spin cyclist. This person's self-talk tends to be more emotive, more focused on managing or trying to avoid threat, and negative self-judgments. There is a significant gap between actual effort and perceived effort, meaning that while reactive individuals perceive they are working hard, their doubting and self-protective self-talk acts to make them push less hard and give up on efforts more quickly.

In Figure 12.2, the same spin class workout plays out differently. With thinking that is observant, responsive, and less reactive, exertion sensations are interpreted more accurately, with less emotionality. As a result, this cyclist is better able to monitor the actual experience, pushing closer to full effort. Note the smaller gap between actual and perceived intensity of effort. By simply observing and responding, this cyclist is expending less cognitive energy, communicating less, and is likely getting a better workout.

Back in my own spin class experience, as my breathing rate goes up and my legs start to feel the effects of high-intensity effort, I have learned, paradoxically, to get calmer and quieter in my head. Less self-talk, more simply noticing. I can almost hear my brain begging me to stop, telling me that I can't do this, warning me that something bad will happen. (I have noticed the brain never makes good on these threats, by the way.) And it is in the mental space that comes from this interested introspection that I have discovered that, actually,

I can work way harder than my brain was warning against. Is it easy? No way. Does it take practice? You betcha. Is it tolerable? Yes, and getting more so all the time, which allows me to push harder.

So while I'd be lying if I said I'm having fun, per se, my hard efforts have gone from brutal to actually interesting. This is the same path elite athletes take on the road to achieving their own goals. When you can learn to override psychological discomfort, even physical pain (safely, and with a doctor's OK, as necessary), then you're that much closer to your own triumphs, too.

Using Visualisation to Prepare for Tough Challenges

Once you have soothed your brain and calmed any anticipatory reactivity as much as you can, your imagination can be harnessed to help you better prepare for what's to come. Neuroscience has shown that when we mentally prepare to do something by visualizing the task to come, the same visual receptor cells that perceive the sensations of sight when we actually see something are firing. That is, our brains do not make a distinction between our imaginings and the experience of seeing in how they process our visual experiences.

When I help athletes visualize, the key variables are the vividness and the controllability they are able to bring to what they see in their mind's eye. *Vividness* translates into the degree of detail and saturation of the image with the goal to increase that as much as possible. *Controllability* is what it sounds like—the ability to control the image, to have the visualization play out the way you want it to. While not everyone can visualize equally well, these are qualities that can improve with practice. Visualisations can come from an internal or external perspective, with some athletes favouring the sense that they are seeing the situation unfold as if it was from their own eyes—the internal perspective—and others liking to see a situation from an external perspective, as if they were seeing themselves on TV.

Rulon Gardner is the USA Greco-Roman wrestler who scored one of the biggest upsets in Olympic history when he beat Aleksandr Karelin in the 2000 Olympics. At the time, Karelin was the overwhelming favourite to win the gold, having gone undefeated for the past 13 years (yes, years) and who, until that Olympic final, had not dropped a single point in the Olympic competition.

Rulon became a student of Karelin. Rulon's brother, Reinhart, put it this way:

> He studied all the videotape of Karelin's career. He saw things. Karelin was not quite so strong now. He could be gassed—if you were in top condition you could run him out of energy. [Rulon] learned all these things and visualized himself taking advantage. He was focused on beating the world's best wrestler.

In the third and final period of their match, Gardner saw the true benefits of his own mental preparation as he perceived Karelin grow increasingly frustrated and confused by his own lack of progress. Gardner realized that Karelin simply had not prepared for this possibility and was able to take competitive advantage, winning the match and the Olympic gold medal in overtime, 1-0.

Visualization is a proven tool, but only if you engage in it. It's mental hard work to imagine, over and over, the details of what you want to have happen. It's even more mentally draining to imagine those scenarios you don't want to have happen, and what you will do when they do. I liken athletes' dislike of this practice to that universal sense of distaste we have when our auto insurance premiums come up for renewal. No one likes to pay for insurance. But when they need that insurance payout, it's a different story.

A case in point: On the day of the final for the sport of skeleton—one of the sliding sports, like bobsled and luge—at the 2002 Winter Olympics, athletes woke up to near-blizzard conditions. Snow on the track acts as a brake for sleds, impacting the lightest athletes the most. First-time US Olympian Tristan Gale was one of the lightest, and for her, the weather initially spelled doom. She and I worked throughout the morning of the competition to first reduce her reactivity and relax into this unfortunate but uncontrollable reality. She then focused her attention on what she would do by visualizing herself navigating each turn under various track conditions, from smooth to snowy. Fortunately for her, a native of Park City, Utah, the Olympic track had been her home track since it was built, and few athletes had spent nearly as much time understanding its terrain. Gale credited her on-the-day visualization with bolstering her ability to let her track knowledge and driving instincts take over, winning her a gold medal.

In this chapter, we established the idea that not all effort is created equal, distinguished between clean and dirty effort, and hopefully made the case that, if offered the choice, we want to "clean up" our efforts. Interestingly, what most often gets in the way is how we think about the challenge at hand. We learned about the value of accurately perceiving the challenge for what it is, no more and no less, and how to help the brain learn to be less reactive in the face of adversity and pain. We finished up with the power of visualization as a way to see challenge ahead of time and practice our response.

KEY TAKEAWAYS

✓ How we perceive challenges is worth unpacking as we explore ways to make our own high-performance challenges less painful and build grit.

✓ Not all efforts are created equal.

✓ When our minds make our efforts harder than they have to be, that's dirty effort. Just as impure fuel hurts an engine over time, our dirty efforts can get the job done but can exact a cost.

✓ When, in contrast, our minds work together with the challenges on offer, our efforts can become cleaner, feel easier, and we can sustain them for longer periods of time.

✓ Insights leading to cleaner effort include the following:
  ◦ Less is more. The mental side of clean effort means

being in touch with reality as it is, facing, without reactivity, the sensations of fatigue and pain with balanced attention and a sense of detached curiosity.

- Resist both the urge to hate the challenge or, conversely, try to pretend it's of no consequence. Either strategy wastes some of your finite emotional resources. Better to focus on what you need to do physically and mentally to prepare for and execute that plan.

- Soothe your brain with nonreactivity. Change the overly dramatic reactive narrative into a matter-of-fact and accurate reporting of events.

✓ Visualize challenges ahead of time to prepare your mind and body for what to expect, and to practice your response.

TO SUM UP

Sometimes, our gritty determination *is* enough to get us across the line and able to deliver on those most challenging efforts and outcomes. This book wasn't written for those times. Instead, this book has focused on how we can think, plan, and behave better to achieve more of the right stuff with less effort in the midst of uncertainty and change.

We learned to recognize when too much grit can be problematic. We discovered evolutionary truths about the human condition that have the potential to undermine performance, as well as some mindset tools to counteract our instinctive patterning. As well, we leaned into uncertainty, exploring how passion and its close but more durable cousin, purpose, can provide a useful internal foundation from which to make better decisions and choices. We saw how putting our purpose into action through service serves others as well as ourselves.

We finished up by looking at effort—the way in which our grit shows up in our behaviour. We learned how to identify when perseverance may not be the right choice, as well as the ins and outs of better, smarter quitting, and concluded with an understanding of the clean-effort mindset.

The Covid pandemic inspired this book, as I watched how

it upended so much of our tried-and-true ways of operating. But my gut tells me that the only constant going forward is that change and uncertainty are here to stay. As a result, those performers who can recognize their current reality quickly and accurately, adapt and adjust the most nimbly, with the least drama, will have the competitive advantage. As well, the mindset, purpose, and effort-related insights and skills outlined in this book can and should be a perennial part of everyone's contemporary high-performance mindset toolbox.

An Epilogue of Note

As I was wrapping up this book, I received a call from Scott Brennan, the rowing athlete whose stories of self-awareness, pain, going from grit to overgrit, and his philosophy about how to reinterpret grit figured prominently in this book.

Scott wanted to let me know about an unexpected turn of events fuelled by advances in medical imaging techniques that led him to recently revisit the site of his long-ago bout with septic arthritis. I'll let him tell it:

> To my shock, there was no joint left on imaging—just solid bone, the joint space completely obliterated by the infection and entirely fused together. Perhaps it's better nobody knew about that at the time, including me. I might have talked myself out of an Olympic gold medal.
>
> It had a funny sense of closing the loop in a way, though. . . . This illness originally granted me the mental perspective to do what I

needed to do, but perhaps once it was done, the permanent phys-
ical changes it left in my body would be the very thing to take it all
away again too. It could be easy to feel resentful and bitter about
that fate. I have to admit that at different times as I struggled
with injury and the perceived injustice of forced retirement, both
of those emotions have been present to varying degrees, but the
mortality I brushed up against as a teenager puts the futility of
those emotions in stark relief: nothing is forever—especially you.
It was going to end some time; just be thankful you got to do it
at all.

I understand that many would regard the illness I went through
and the experience it encompassed as traumatic and highly
negative. Certainly taken on its own, that is the accurate way to
describe it. But our experiences can never exist on their own, only
in the greater context of our entire lives, and in that regard my
experience of suffering has paid unforeseen dividends through-
out my careers as both athlete and medical doctor, ultimately
extending to help colour the way I view life itself, not least my
deeply abiding gratitude that I still have life to continue reflecting
on. (Thank you, modern medicine.) Just like we rush to envy the
good fortune of those who win lottery fortunes yet don't stay to
see the chaos it can bring, we can be prone to immediately judge
the most challenging moments of our lives in a deeply negative
light before the fruits of our suffering have been given time to
grow into wisdom.

Huge and heartfelt thanks to Scott for his willingness to
share this most recent chapter in his saga. He wrapped up the

conundrum well: life hands us lessons and insights, but it's up to us to determine how to use them. And sometimes even our hard-won lessons aren't always fit for purpose or can outlive their usefulness. Yet, life goes on with new challenges to learn from and insights to be gained. I believe Scott would agree that it's not about *what* happens to us but *how* we cope, come to terms with, and learn from those challenges that informs a better, even Olympic-gold-winning life.

I wish you, dear reader, the very best in all your Journeys Worth Taking—gritty *and* otherwise—and hope this book filled in some blanks for how to get where you want to go more easily and efficiently.

APPENDIX: CORE VALUES

- Achievement
- Adventure
- Authenticity
- Authority
- Autonomy
- Balance
- Beauty
- Boldness
- Compassion
- Challenge
- Citizenship
- Community
- Competency
- Contribution
- Creativity
- Curiosity
- Determination
- Fairness
- Faith
- Fame
- Friendships
- Fun
- Growth
- Happiness
- Honesty
- Humour
- Influence
- Inner Harmony
- Justice
- Kindness
- Knowledge
- Leadership
- Learning
- Love
- Loyalty
- Meaningful Work
- Openness
- Optimism
- Peace
- Pleasure
- Poise
- Popularity
- Recognition
- Religion
- Reputation
- Respect
- Responsibility
- Security
- Self-Respect
- Service
- Spirituality
- Stability
- Status
- Success
- Trustworthiness
- Wealth
- Wisdom

REFERENCES

Beilock, S. (2010). *Choke: What the secrets of the brain reveal about getting it right when you have to*. New York: Simon & Schuster.

Brewer, J. (2021). *Unwinding anxiety: Train your brain to heal your mind*. New York: Penguin Random House.

Clear, J. (2018). *Atomic habits: Tiny changes, remarkable results*. New York: Century-Trade.

Dubner, S. (2011). The upside of quitting. Freakonomics podcast. https://freakonomics.com/podcast/new-freakonomics-radio-podcast-the-upside-of-quitting

Duckworth, A. (2016). *Grit: The power of passion and perseverance*. New York: Scribner.

Epstein, D. (2019). *Range: How generalists triumph in a specialized world*. New York: Riverhead Books.

Eurich, T. (2018). *Insight: The surprising truth about how others see us, how we see ourselves, and why the answers matter more than we think*. New York: Currency Press.

Finalist dies at World Sauna event in Finland. (2010). https://www.bbc.com/news/world-europe-1090469

The Future of the World Sauna Championships. (n.d.). https://www.heinola.fi/NR/rdonlyres/79A6874F-1F8E-4011-89BD-E233DB4B3605/0/Sauna_Championships.pdf

Godin, S. (2007). *The dip: The little book that teaches you when to quit (and when to stick)*. New York: Penguin.

Goleman, D. (1995). *Emotional intelligence: Why it can matter more than IQ*. New York: Random House/Bantam Books.

Hill, P., & Turiano, N. (2014). Purpose in life as a predictor of mortality across adulthood. *Psychological Science*. doi: 10.1177/0956797614531799

Jachimowicz, J. (2019, October). 3 reasons it's so hard to follow your passion. *Harvard Business Review*. https://hbr.org/2019/10/3-reasons-its-so-hard-to-follow-your-passion

Kahneman, D., & Tversky, A. (1979). Prospect theory: An analysis of decision under risk. *Econometrica, 47*, 263–291.

Killingsworth, M. A., & D. T. Gilbert. (2010, Nov. 11). A wandering mind is an unhappy mind. *Science, 330*(6006): 932–932. doi:10.1126/science.1192439

Leider, R. (2015). *The power of purpose: Find meaning, live longer, better.* San Francisco: Berrett-Koehler.

Madore, K. P., & Wagner, A. D. (2019). Multicosts of multitasking. *Cerebrum: The Dana Forum on Brain Science, 2019*, cer-04-19.

McClellan, M. D. (2017, April 25). Dan Jansen: Unbreakable—The Dan Jansen interview. https://www.fifteenminuteswith.com/2017/04/25/dan-jansen-unbreakable/

Neff, K. (2011). *Self-compassion: Stop beating yourself up and leave insecurity behind.* New York: Morrow.

Nietzsche, F. W., & Hollingdale, R. J. (1878/1986). *Human, all too human: A book for free spirits.* New York: Cambridge University Press.

Oettingen, G. (1996). Positive fantasy and motivation. In P. M. Gollwitzer & J. A. Bargh (Eds.), *The psychology of action: Linking cognition and motivation to behavior* (pp. 236–259). New York: Guilford.

Pearce, N. (2019, October). Why purpose, not passion, should guide young professionals. *Harvard Business Review*. https://hbr.org/2019/10/why-purpose-not-passion-should-guide-young-professionals

Phillips, A. (1988, Feb. 15). Day of tragedy for speed skater ends with fall. *Washington Post*.

Pressfield, S. (2012). *Turning pro: Tap your inner power and create your life's work.* Black Irish Books

Rotella, R. J., Gansneder, B., Ojala, D., & Billing, J. (1980). Cognitions and coping strategies of elite skiers: An exploratory study of young developing athletes. *Journal of Sport Psychology, 2*, 350–354.

Rubinstein, J. S., Meyer, D. E., & Evans, J. E. (2001). Executive control of cognitive processes in task switching. *Journal of Experimental Psychology: Human Perception and Performance, 27,* 763–797.

Schawbel, D. (2017, Jan. 9). Angela Duckworth: A passion is developed more than it is discovered. *Forbes.* https://www.forbes.com/sites/danschawbel/2017/01/09/angela-duckworth-a-passion-is-developed-more-than-it-is-discovered/

Shaw, G. B. (2008). *Man and superman: A comedy and a philosophy.* McLean, VA: IndyPublish.com

Taylor, S. E. (2006). Tend and befriend: Biobehavioral bases of affiliation under stress. *Current Directions in Psychological Science, 15*(6), 273–277. doi: 10.1111/j.1467-8721.2006.00451.x

Wallace, D. F. (2005). *This is water.* Commencement speech at Kenyon College, Gambier, OH.

Wilson, T. D., Reinhard, D. A., Westgate, E. C., Gilbert, D. T., Ellerbeck, N., Hahn, C., Brown, C. L., & Shaked, A. (2014). Just think: The challenges of the disengaged mind. *Science, 345*(6192), 75–77. https://doi.org/10.1126/science.1250830

ABOUT THE AUTHOR

As an experienced Olympic performance psychologist, mindset educator, and keynote speaker, Kirsten Peterson understands how to work with teams and individuals to make healthier high performance happen. She also helps us overcome the ways we inadvertently get in the way of our best work, including—just maybe—overindexing on our grit!

Having been a senior sport psychologist for the US Olympic Committee and head of Performance Psychology at the Australian Institute of Sport, Kirsten spent decades helping Olympic athletes, coaches, and teams. She melds this experience with expertise in neuroscience and mindfulness into an informed approach that teaches people how to work better with their brains and minds for improved well-being, interpersonal connection, and more sustainable performance.

Kirsten graduated from Union College in Schenectady, NY, USA, with a bachelor's in psychology, and received her master's in sport psychology and doctorate in counselling psychology from the University of Illinois–Urbana, IL, USA. She is a certified executive coach and meditation teacher.

Kirsten works with individuals interested in unlocking their next level, leaders seeking to inspire more from themselves and their teams, and teams needing a healthy high-performance culture reboot. She can be contacted at kirsten@kirstenpetersonconsulting.com.